Introduction

English writers have a way of invoking paternal
imagery when thinking of Chaucer. "As he is the
Father of English Poetry," wrote John Dryden, "so
I hold him in the same Degree of Veneration as the
Grecians held Homer, or the Romans Virgil" – or
the Italians Dante, he might have added.

G. K. Chesterton took the figure even further.
"The Medieval word for a Poet, was a Maker," he
wrote, and "there was never a man who was more
of a maker than Chaucer. He made a national
language; he came very near to making a nation.
At least without him it would probably have
been either so fine a language or so great a nation.
Shakespeare and Milton were the greatest sons
of their country; but Chaucer was the father of his

country, rather in the manner of George Washington."

A sweeping claim, maybe, but with a nucleus of truth. Chaucer really was a kind of English founding father. He didn't invent the language for literature but, unlike his contemporary John Gower, he chose it as his only literary language, thus limiting his fame across Europe, where authorship was assessed on literary production in Latin, French and Italian. Chaucer could read and write in all three, but when it came to his creative writing, he put his energy into exploiting and developing the English he was born with, vastly expanding its vocabulary to the extent of around 2,000 words, its rhetoric, its levels of register – not to mention its prosody.

And *The Canterbury Tales* is where it happened, more so than in the dream poems like *The Book of the Duchess*, the translation of Boethius's *Consolation of Philosophy* or the long verse romance *Troilus and Criseyde,* all of which worked within continental conventions.

The Canterbury Tales was truly original. Giovanni Boccaccio's *Decameron* had used the same format of many stories told within a framing narrative, but his interlocutors were all aristocratic and in the same place, a country house outside Florence. Chaucer's narrators, pilgrims on the road to Canterbury, span a broad range of social levels, from a knight, down through a wealthy landowner, a merchant, a miller and minor church officials.

They are brought to life in the General Prologue

by vivid descriptions of their clothing, bodily appearance and behaviour – and later in their tales through the wide variety of English vernacular they voice. These are the raw materials out of which Chaucer not only produces comedy both coarse and subtle, as well as more general social satire, but also more remarkably explores and develops themes that go well beyond Boccaccio's, like the condition of the church, the conflict between fate and free will, experience as against authority, and – at a deeper level – what it is that constitutes authority, whether in the Bible or the conventions of courtly-love romance.

It's no wonder that to many authors this comprehensive panorama of English types, voices and concerns should have seemed to be both a model to be admired and also a founding statement of national identity. From long before Dryden and Chesterton – in fact only a generation after his death – Chaucer was already being revered as the Aureate Laureate by poets like John Lydgate and Thomas Hoccleve. By 1478, even though the work had circulated only in manuscript, the printer William Caxton thought it to be such an English monument that he invested a fortune in time and money to publish *The Canterbury Tales* as the first ever book in English to be printed in England. It has never been out of print since.

The nature of
The Canterbury Tales

Thirty-four travellers of varying classes and occupations meet at the Tabard Inn in Southwark, just south of London Bridge, the night before they are due to set out on horseback on a pilgrimage to the shrine of Saint Thomas à Becket in Canterbury Cathedral. At dinner the Tabard's landlord, their host Harry Bailly, suggests that he join them on their journey and that they divert themselves by telling stories along the way. Each pilgrim will tell two stories going to Canterbury and a further two on the way back. He or she who tells the "Tales of best sentence and most solas" [deepest meaning and most delight] (798), will be given a dinner at the others' expense.

That's the context, the so-called frame narrative of *The Canterbury Tales*. In the event only 24 tales get told, along with 20 prologues, including 'The General Prologue' that sets the scene. Most are verse narratives. Some are posed as fictional – that is, designated explicitly as tales or stories. Others, like the 'Wife of Bath's Prologue', or the Friar's and Pardoner's Prologues, are narratives drawn from the life of the teller – supposedly factual accounts, telling the other pilgrims something about the Narrator's customary practice or profession.

Only two tales are set in prose. The first is 'The Tale of Melibee', told by Chaucer's own persona after he has tried his hand at the verse 'Tale of Sir Topas' and had his efforts dismissed by the host:

"By God," quod he, "for pleynly, at a word,
Thy drasty [crappy] rhyming is not worth a
toord [turd].
Lat se wher thou kanst tellen aught in geeste
[alliterative verse]
Or telle in prose somwhat at the leeste [at least]."
[929-933]

This is clearly a joke, since the very same Chaucer – not as a character in the action but *in propria persona* – is the highly adept poet behind the rest of *The Tales*, including Harry Bailly's own derisive comments.

The prose of 'The Parson's Tale' is no joke, though. It reads as a sermon or treatise on penitence, and it comes at the end of *The Tales,* just before Chaucer's Retraction, his palinode, in which he begs his readers to pray for him, that Christ might "foryeve me my *giltes* [sins]" specifically for having translated 'The Romance of the Rose', and for having composed 'Troilus and Criseyde', 'The Book of the Duchess', 'The Parliament of Fowls' and *The Canterbury Tales* themselves.

Palinodes, or retractions, were not uncommon in medieval literature, but for an author to renounce all his major works might be said to push the convention to its extreme. And taken together – as it should be – with the serious prose of 'The Parson's Tale', the retraction seems to suggest that prose is the proper medium for truth, and that verse and fiction – especially in the service of romance or social satire – were ultimately frivolous in their stimulation of laughter and the fancy: when spiritual reality had finally to be faced and told, farewell metaphor, symbolism and allegory, farewell irony, farewell stories – moral and diverting, humane and humorous – drawn from the classics, from legends and from contemporary life.

If Chaucer wished to do penance because he couldn't un-write those great works of his, we can at least give thanks that his remorse came too late to recall them (not that he could; they had already been widely circulated in numerous manuscripts). He wasn't the first author to use the English language for literary purposes – others included his near contemporaries John Gower, William Langland and the anonymous author of 'Pearl' and 'Sir Gawain and the Green Knight' – but he was the first to deploy its full potential to produce both "sentence" [meaning] and "solas" [delight]. At a time when Latin was used in government and the law courts, and French thought most appropriate for romances of courtly love, Chaucer seems almost to have invented the vernacular for literature, exploiting its wide lexical range running from Latinic right through to Germanic sources, now using the French end of the spectrum for the great epics of sentiment like 'Troilus and Criseyde' and 'The Knight's Tale', now relishing the common tongue drawn from the Anglo-Saxon for exchanges between the pilgrims, and for *fabliaux* like 'The Miller's Tale' and 'The Reeve's Tale'. Best of all, he often brought the two levels together, side by side, for maximum comic and moral effect.

Highly varied as it is in style, substance and type of story, *The Canterbury Tales* is far from systematic in its layout. Giovanni Boccaccio's *Il Decamerone* (*ca* 1353), which Chaucer almost certainly knew and used as a source, is also a collection of stories set within a framing narrative. Instead of pilgrims of all classes, Boccaccio's storytellers are ten young aristocrats – seven women and three men – who escape the bubonic plague raging in Florence by removing to an empty villa in Fiesole for two weeks. Apart from one day per week for chores, and the various holy days when no one works at all, they must tell ten stories, one each in each of the ten days remaining (the title comes from Greek *deka*, ten, plus *hemera*, day, together with an Italian suffix suggesting "big" – hence "ten long days"). And so *Il Decamerone* is indeed a collection of exactly 100 stories.

By contrast the structure of *The Canterbury Tales* is very ragged. First of all, how many pilgrims are there? In 'The General Prologue' the Narrator,

Chaucer's persona, says there were "welnyne and twenty in a compaignye/Of sondry folk" (24-25). In fact, there are 34, including the four guildsmen (a haberdasher, a carpenter, a weaver, a dyer and a tapestry maker (361-362)), the Canon, who runs away when he thinks his yeoman is about to reveal his dirty secrets (702), the Host and Chaucer's persona.

Of these, only 22 tell a tale, including the two told by Chaucer's persona, the aborted verse 'Tale of Sir Thopas' and the prose 'The Tale of Melibee'. So instead of 136 tales, which we would get if all 34 pilgrims told two going and two coming back, or even 116, if the narrator's tally of 29 travellers were accurate, we have just 24. The failure to realise the Host's grand plan, together with the narrator's confusion about how many pilgrims are in the party, contribute to the general sense of haphazardness – or call it fluidity – as if the structure of the work was answering the accidents of everyday life, rather than being driven by an abstract formula in the hands of some overbearing author figure.

Yet for all that, there is little of that novelistic realism of everyday life in *The Canterbury Tales*. Character is not much developed, so there is little interest in the individual's psychology such as we get in novels. In *The Canterbury Tales* the nearest we get to complex characters are Dorigen in 'The Franklin's Tale' and the Wife of Bath – both women, to be sure, but still a long way from the female protagonists whose development – whether emotional, intellectual, moral or humane – forms the plot of novels like *Emma* (1815), *Middlemarch* (1874) or *The Portrait of a Lady* (1881). And what look at first like realistic characters are really more like caricatures or stereotypes – whether comic or threatening, beatific or bestial – drawn not so much from "real life" as from popular social satires of the three estates of clergy, nobility and common people.

Indeed in places Chaucer seems to have been quite deliberate in suppressing character. In Boccaccio's *La Teseide* (1340-1341), Chaucer's source for 'The Knight's Tale', the personalities of the two young knights who fight for the love of Emily are quite clearly distinguished. To quote Derek Pearsall's life of Chaucer, Arcite is "the wholly admirable hero who is unlucky, and Palamon the runner-up who gets the prize when the winner is disqualified". In 'The Knight's Tale', by contrast, "it is hard to tell them apart, and neither behaves well".

So *The Canterbury Tales* are not an early form of novel, or even a collection of short stories. It's not just their (predominate) verse form that sets them off from modern fiction, but also their relationship to reality. Early theorists of the novel repeatedly defined the form as a reaction against the romance. Hence Clara Reeve in *The Progress of Romance* (1785):

> The Romance is an heroic fable, which treats
> of fabulous persons and things. The Novel is a
> picture of real life and manners, and of the times
> in which it is written. The Romance in lofty
> and elevated language, describes what never
> happened nor is likely to happen. The novel gives
> a familiar relation of such things, as pass every
> day before our eyes... until we are affected by the
> joys and distresses, of the persons in the story, as
> if they were our own.

"Joys and distresses" so lifelike, it's as if we owned them. That's why generations of readers have talked about "identifying with" Elizabeth Bennett or Huck Finn, or other characters in a novel. The

PILGRIMAGES

Before the Reformation pilgrimages were common among all people, poor and rich alike. Apart from Canterbury, popular English places of pilgrimage included the shrines of St Swithun in Winchester, Our Lady of Walsingham in Norfolk and St Cuthbert in Durham.

If the poor had to keep to local travel, the better off could afford to go further afield. The Wife of Bath could tick off even more foreign pilgrimages than she could husbands – to holy places in Boulogne, Cologne, St Peter's in Rome, to the

novel is about people we can recognize, people remarkable not for their heroics, but for their sensitivity, perception, their ability to learn. Its action is un-melodramatic. It takes place in an ordinary time and place, not in some never-never land. And that's also why the "persons" in *The Canterbury Tales* aren't like characters in a novel.

But above all, as its name proclaims, the novel is *new*. It tells a new story, one not told before. By contrast all the tales in *The Canterbury Tales* – except the Parson's, which isn't a "tale" as such – are derived from originals ranging from Ovid's *Metamorphoses,* Aesop's *Fables* and the Epistles of St Paul to 'The Romance of the Rose', Boccaccio's *Filocolo* and *Decameron* and 'The Romance of Guy of Warwick'. As Ian Watt pointed out in his classic *The Rise of the Novel* (1963), this novelty of the

---

shrine of St James of Compostella in Galicia, and to the Holy Land, no fewer than three times. ('The General Prologue', 463-466). But her wealth and worldly experience didn't prevent her from mixing with the less well off on the more humble trip to the popular shrine of St Thomas à Becket in Canterbury cathedral.

Did pilgrims just go along for the jaunt, as on a sort-of medieval village coach tour? No doubt the urge for social cohesion played a part, but individual devotion was a strong motive too. As 'The General Prologue' makes clear, pilgrimages weren't just something you did because you yearned to visit "straunge strondes" [foreign shores] when the weather improved the roads in spring, but something you did, "with ful devout corage" [spiritual

novel has to do with differing medieval and modern concepts of nature:

> Early novelists... are the first great writers in our literature who did not take their plots from mythology, history, legend, or previous literature. In this they differ from Chaucer, Spenser, Shakespeare, and Milton, for instance, who, like the writers of Greece and Rome, habitually used traditional plots; and who did so, in the last analysis, because they accepted the general premise of their times that, since Nature is essentially complete and unchanging, its records, whether scriptural, legendary, or historical, constitute a definitive repertoire of human experience.

The Canterbury Tales proclaim this idea of nature

---

feeling], "The hooly blisful martir for to seke" (13, 22, 17).

What would they find when they got to their destination? A richly decorated reliquary, strewn with votive offerings from other pilgrims who had sought the saint's intercession. Becket's shrine, raised on a marble plinth, was a casket covered in gold, silver and precious jewels.

The more sumptuous decorations had been donated by wealthy worshippers, some of them aristocratic, but ordinary pilgrims left their own gifts, and bought pilgrim badges to wear on their way home. This income from pilgrims largely paid for the Cathedral's rebuilding.

What would they do when they reached their destination? They might seek

from the very first lines of 'The General Prologue':

Whan that Aprill with his shoures soote
[showers sweet]
The droghte of Marche hath perced to the roote,
[root]
And bathed every veyne in swich licour,
Of which vertu engendred is the flour;
Whan Zephirus eek with his sweete breeth
Inspired hath in every holt [wood] and heeth
[heath]
The tendre croppes, and the yonge sonne
Hath in the Ram [Zodiac sign] his half cours
yronne;
And smale foweles maken melodye,
That slepen al the nyght with open ye [eye]
(So priketh hem [spurs them] Nature in hir

the saint's intercession – anything ranging from a safe journey to success in a business venture – but above all in a cure or something else pertaining to health, since Canterbury was renowned as a place of healing. But they came not always to ask, as 'The General Prologue' makes clear, but also to thank the saint "That hem [them] hath holpen whan that they were seeke" (18), for a boon already granted.

After the dissolution of the monasteries from 1536 to 1541, pilgrimage fell rapidly into desuetude as a popular pastime. In 1538, Henry VIII wittily summoned the long dead Thomas à Becket to court on a charge of high treason, then ordered the destruction of his shrine after he failed to turn up, trousering the proceeds for the treasury ■

> corages, [spirits])
> Thanne longen folk to goon on pilgrimages,
> And palmeres for to seken [seek] straunge
>   stroundes [shores]
> To ferne halwes [far off shrines], kowthe
>   [known] in sondry londes,
> And specially from every shires ende
> Of Engelond to Caunterbury they wende,
> The hooly blisful martir for to seke,
> That hem hath holpen, when that they were
>   seeke [sick].
>   [1-18]

Here is nature as process, assisted by a mythological figure (Zephirus, the west wind that blows in spring), re-animating the flowers, birds and young crops. The people too are re-vivified, motivated by the season when the roads begin to dry out, by their love of company and their gratitude to the "hooly blisful martir", to go on their springtime pilgrimages.

Though a process, however, the annual natural cycle is also unchanging; though it goes through seasons as the sun rolls through the Ram and other signs of the zodiac, it does so every year. The whole long verse paragraph is framed as a general proposition: this is what people do, and have always done in the spring. Their religious motives are in turn motivated by Nature, because they are all a part of it; Nature is God's creation.

Because prompted by Nature, the caricatures in 'The General Prologue' are also naturalised. The Knight who "loved chivalrie" (45), the Prioress who would weep if she saw a mouse caught in a trap (145), the Monk who "lovede venerie" (hunting and sexual adventure) and who kept well away from the cloister (166, 185), the wanton, merry friar, who "knew the tavernes wel in every toun" (240) – all these conform to type. Satire is softened by tradition. As Derek Pearsall writes, the pilgrims "have all the faults of the traditional victims of estates satire, but they are not openly castigated for them; the faults seem to be part of the pattern of behaviour appropriate to their professions and to their relation to the money economy".

With Nature governing things as they are – and always have been and will be – there is no need for the novelty of the novel. New characters, original plots – these require authorial effort and space in the text to establish, to make believable through details of realistic setting and psychology. Relieved of the burden of novelty, uncharged with the responsibility of making things new, *The Canterbury Tales* are free to explore abstract themes like the moral authority of the Church in England, and the philosophical distinctions between fortune and providence, fate and free will, letter and spirit. In 'The Pardoner's Prologue and Tale', there is even room for a crucial aesthetic conundrum: how can an immoral man tell a moral tale? What is it about fiction that allows it to stand up even when told by a self-confessedly corrupt narrator? Above all, to what extent does the tale depend on authority and its interpretation – on the various models set by the classics, by scripture and by feudal society as mediated by clerics, scholars and other licensed – or self-proclaimed "experts"?

What are *The Canterbury Tales* about?

Early 20th-century critics like George Lyman Kittredge would be unable to answer this question. *The Canterbury Tales* aren't *about* anything, they would say; they simply *are*. They are a dramatic presentation of the human comedy, a procession of more-or-less realistic characters, reflecting their own vivid personalities and the social dynamics of their age. The only topics to be found in the work, therefore, are the ones voiced and debated by the pilgrims themselves, their own concerns as explored in dramatic debate.

Chief among these subjects, thought Kittredge, was the debate about marriage – specifically over whether the husband or the wife should be dominant. In a landmark article published in 1912 he traced a debate beginning with the Wife of Bath, who argued for the wife's supremacy. She is

Geoffrey Chaucer, 1343-1400
From the book Gallery Of Portraits *published in London in 1833*

answered by 'The Clerk's Tale', the story of patient Griselda who endures all manner of deprivation and humiliation at the hands of her husband, emerging from her ordeals as the same faithful, true wife. 'The Merchant's Tale' calls upon a bewildering array of authorities to prove the fallibility of women, as exemplified by a young wife who cheats on her elderly husband. Finally, 'The Franklin's Tale' is supposed to resolve the question of *maistrie* in marriage by posing a relationship in which the husband would be "servant in love, and lord in mariage" (792).

Even those looking for a meaning beyond the dramatic dialogue between the characters would find it hard to say what *The Canterbury Tales* are about. How could we expect a common theme to emerge from 20 prologues and 24 tales voiced by people of all classes and most occupations, in tones ranging from solemnity to slapstick, differing widely in length, levels of diction and seriousness, with story lines embracing everything from courtly love and chivalric conflict to two students, who in order to work revenge on a cheating miller, seduce his wife and daughter?

If a common theme is hard to find, the tales do raise various topics along their way. The condition of the Church in England, for example, and especially the integrity of its mendicant orders, gets several airings, beginning in 'The General Prologue', with the narrator's ironic approval of the Monk:

And I seyde his opinioun was good.
What [Why] sholde he studie, and make
                hymselven wood [mad, crazy]
Upon a book in cloystre alwey to poure,
                [pore over]
Or swynken [work] with his handes and laboure
As Austyn bit [St Augustine bid]?
How shal the world be served?
Let Austyn have his swynk to hym reserved!
                [183-188]

The issue of the morality of fiction – whether a
moral tale loses its force if told by an immoral man
– is neatly posed in 'The Pardoner's Prologue':

Thus kan I preche agayn [against] that
                same vice
Which that I use [practice], and that is avarice.
                [427-428]

... and recurs when the venal Monk tells his tale
moralising the deaths of famous men.

A more general theme, raised throughout
The Tales, is the very language in which they
are written – not the question of whether the
vernacular is suitable for literature, but whether
any post-Edenic language can be used for sacred
topics. Discussing the castrated Pardoner's "partial
objects" (his relics, but also his sexual parts)
brought in to "fill... the loss of an original ideal",

Carolyn Dinshaw sets out that widespread medieval belief, as explored in the writings of St Augustine among others, that language had fallen along with man's fall from grace. Although the Incarnation had redeemed fallen language along with fallen humanity, and "restored the word to the Word", nevertheless, language remained partial, fragmentary, unstable, unfit to express the divine.

So the text generates lots of interest in *how* people speak – and not just false preachers like the Pardoner – especially their self-consciously rhetorical flights, which often contrast with other aspects (including the moral intent) of their discourse. The gap between the letter and the spirit is a recurring topic in *The Canterbury Tales.*

Then there is fate and free will. "All Chaucer's serious poetry seems to me to be preoccupied with the question of free will and the manner in which it is possessed by human beings," Derek Pearsall has written. Certainly the issue is discussed (on one level) by the Wife of Bath, and (on another, more elevated "philosophical" level) when Dorigen laments her fate in 'The Franklin's Tale' (865-890). The apparently irreconcilable conflict between the two concepts – will and fate – forms the backbone of the tragedy in 'The Knight's Tale'.

We have to wait for the Nun's Priest's beast fable to hear the dilemma resolved in terms that Chaucer got from translating Boethius – that "fate" is a pagan concept, and that the Christian

God's providence sees all without constraining the free will of humankind – before the issue is dismissed as irrelevant to the story of a cock being stalked by a fox (1233-1252).

Above all, repeatedly, and involving most of the tales, is the question of how we come to know something. This is not so much a theme as an issue, foregrounded again and again, as the narrators draw attention to what they know (and don't know), and their authority for saying so.

"There are known knowns; there are things we know that we know," as Donald Rumsfeld, the US Secretary of Defence, famously said in 2002. And, of course, there are "known unknowns; that is to say there are things that we now know we don't know. But there are also unknown unknowns – there are things we do not know we don't know."

Sometimes the knowledge or lack of it seems trivial, as when the Narrator in 'The General Prologue' admits he doesn't know the Merchant's name (284). He doesn't know the Shipman's either (though he doesn't say so; maybe this is an unknown unknown), but he does know that his barge is called the Maudelayne (410).

Other declarations of ignorance are fraught with consequences for the story, as when Palamon in 'The Knight's Tale' says he doesn't know whether Emily is a woman or a goddess (1101), or for the whole philosophical and spiritual ethos of that tale, when the Knight says of Arcite's soul:

> *His spirit chaunged hous and wente ther,*
> *As I cam nevere, I kan nat tellen wher.*
>
> *[2809-10]*

As for what they know that they know, the pilgrims offer myriad examples in both Prologues and Tales, most of them backed up by some authority or another. Authority, much cited as *auctoritee*, can be defined as the truth of learned tradition in any writings from the past.

Authority ultimately derives from God, of course, but to discern its truth in everyday life was not always straightforward. D. W. Robertson, citing Hugh of St Victor, sets out the problem:

> Things... constitute the 'vox Dei ad homines' the voice of God speaking to men. Whether this voice was heard in the things mentioned in Scripture or in the created world itself, which came to be called 'the book of God's work', it was an enigmatic voice. To find tongues in trees, books in running brooks, Sermons in stones, and good in everything requires not only that fascination of the exterior man for 'painted pomp' be set aside, but also that the reason be prepared to ascend from the visible to the invisible.

But once in the realm of the invisible, you begin to

lose your bearings. To hear God's voice you had to be an acute listener, or reader, and a careful sifter of ambiguity. This, says Kathy Cawsey, means that Chaucer's characters are also readers:

> readers of the world, readers of each other, readers of the stories they themselves tell. These in-the-text readers then become exemplary readers for the out-of-text readers of Chaucer's actual audience. Good readers, those who read according to the dictates of charity, become examples of good hermeneutical practice for Chaucer's real readers, while bad readers, those who read according to worldly desire and cupidity, become examples of how not to read.

This strenuous hermeneutical* enterprise within the text explains why Chaucer's characters – whether knightly, scholarly or otherwise, learned, or humble – are forever referring to authority, be it that of the classics, the Bible and its scholarly interpreters, literary convention like courtly love or just earlier works of literature.

Yet neither Robertson nor Cawsey have quite conveyed the centrality of the practice, how it permeates *The Canterbury Tales*, or the uneasiness with which the characters undertake it – or to put it another way, the extent to which Chaucer so

* that is to say, interpretative.

often foregrounds the problematic of exegesis in the words and acts of his characters. Much of the sentence of *The Canterbury Tales* and much of its comedy comes from how the interpretation of authority is both proclaimed and yet contested, undermined, even satirised.

Indeed, the exegetical project often occupies the centre ground of any dispute between the characters. So the so-called marriage debate seems more to be about which expert you trust – or deploy to establish your argument – than about the experience of marriage itself. As January, the old knight in 'The Merchant's Tale', looks forward to a marriage "so esy and so clene [comfortable and pure]/That in this world it is a paradys", he pauses to reflect that "somme clerkes [scholars] seyn it nys nat so" (1264-1265, 1293). Among these experts is Theophrastus, as excerpted by St Jerome in his *Against Jovinian* (ca. 393 C.E.), who warned against the expense of taking a wife.

Then he goes on for over another hundred lines, citing examples from the Bible of good and bad wives, until he hits on the Stoic philosopher Seneca, who in turn cites Cato, the Roman statesman, that a wife, far from being a cost, will look after the household finances quite well. And so it goes, back and forth. His two brothers offer similarly contrasting views, with Placebo citing Solomon over 40 lines in support, and Justinius

AN ALBERTO GRIMALDI PRODUCTION **"THE CANTERBURY TALES"** : BASED ON THE 'CANTERBURY TALES' BY G. CHAUCER
A FILM BY PIER PAOLO PASOLINI

Pier Paolo Pasolini's The Canterbury Tales, *released in 1972. Produced by Alberto Grimaldi (*The Good, the Bad and the Ugly, *1966,* Last Tango in Paris, *1972,* Gangs of New York, *2002). Pasolini, the notorious poet, novelist, film director, thinker and journalist, was highly rated by American critic Harold Bloom, who included him in his book* The Western Canon.

against, quoting Seneca (again) to the effect that, be careful to whom you entrust your land and cattle. Not that any of this affects January in the slightest; he goes ahead and does what he was planning to do all along, marry the girl.

The Wife of Bath seems at first to depart from this impulse to interpret. Uniquely among the pilgrims, she offers her experience – indeed experience in general – as an antidote to theoretical debates drawn from authority. She does this from the very beginning of her robust defence of women:

> *"Experience, though noon auctoritee*
> *Were in this world, is right ynogh for me*
> *To speke of te wo that is in mariage."*
>
> *[1-3]*

CHAUCER'S RETRACTION AND 'THE PARSON'S TALE'

At the Host's invitation to tell a fable, the Parson responds that he will instead speak in prose. What follows is a long treatise on sin and repentance, an implied rebuke to much that has motivated the other pilgrims, but also "To knytte up al this feeste and make an ende" and to argue that the true pilgrimage is the voyage to "Jerusalem celestial" (46, 51). This leads to a sort-of postscript in which Chaucer begs forgiveness for having written most of the works for

Yet even she can't do so without invoking authority, in however negative a light. A few lines further on she satirises Biblical exegesis, only to wind up doing it herself – citing Genesis 1:22 ("And God blessed them, saying, Be fruitful, and multiply") – when the text suits her purpose:

> *"Men may devyne [conjecture] and glosen*
> *[interpret], up and doun.*
> *But wel I woot [know], expres [clearly],*
> *withoute lye,*
> *God bad us for to wexe [increase] and multiplye;"*
> *[26-28]*

If January and his brothers invoke classical and Biblical authority to no purpose, the Pardoner puts it to pernicious use: to cheat the rich out of their

which he has always been most admired, including *The Canterbury Tales*.

Because 'The Parson's Tale' and Chaucer's retraction seem so out of key with the rest of the book, critics have wondered whether they were really meant to conclude the work, or whether they belong in *The Canterbury Tales* at all. The Explanatory Notes of the Riverside Edition, (pp.

954-955 and 965) summarise these doubts and dispel them.

For Derek Pearsall, it is only in 'The Parson's Tale' that Chaucer "can be said to speak unequivocally from and of the truth of faith". The tale cannot be contained "within any framework of irony or dramatic voicing ... [It] is not merely something to set beside the various kinds of fictionality that have

gold and silver and the poor out of their cheese and wheat (440, 448). His confident sermons (for the rich) in elevated diction, seasoned with a smattering of Latin, and (for the unlearned poor) repeating old stories from folklore are all underpinned by his licence to preach and his writs of indulgence (330, 344, 435-437, 226).

And so the hermeneutic urge threads itself through *The Canterbury Tales*, now asserted, now resisted, usually for selfish gain, or to cover a false position, or just to show off. Nowhere is itch so intense (and intensive) as in Nun's Priest's fable of Chauntecleer and Pertelote. After a nightmare in which he is chased and almost caught by a fox, the rooster asks how he can interpret his dream correctly (2896). His "faire damoysele", the hen Pertelote, tells him to forget it, because Cato said pay no attention to dreams. Ah, but what about the

---

gone before, but a denial of the value of fiction".

As for the retraction, Pearsall says it is "Chaucer's own historical response to the call for penitence, and penitence *now*, which is the imperative logic of the closing paragraphs of the Parson's treatise". It "confirms the passing of artistic into historical consciousness. It is Chaucer's own act of satisfaction..." Hence the revoking, or unwriting, of the Chaucer texts. The truth of Christian doctrine is demonstrated and best served by their non-being.

The idea that 'The Parson's Tale' and the retraction un-make all the fiction that went before them seems a bit extreme, if not downright perverse. Chaucer's retraction is a palinode.

Life of Saint Kenelm, son of Cenwulf, says Chauntecleer, who was murdered shortly after dreaming he would be? Then there's Macrobius's Commentary on Cicero's *Dream of Scipio*, which proves that dreams can be accurate visions of the future (2940-2941, 3110-3119, 3123-3125).

And so it goes on, with at least 11 further citations of authority, drawn from the Bible, or the classics or philosophers, including the Nun's Priest's own digression on the problem of fate and free will, as noted above. Even the fox refers to Boethius and remembers *Burnellus* (or the *Speculum Stultorum*), a 12th-century Latin satire in which a cock takes revenge on a candidate for ordination, crowing so late that he oversleeps and loses his benefice (3294, 3312-3316).

Is 'The Nun's Priest Tale' also a satire? If so, on what? Hardly on the animals, who behave better

Palinodes were a widespread classical and medieval device. They can be found in Saint Augustine's *Retractions*, in the works of the Venerable Bede, Giraldus Cambrensis, Jean de Meun and Andreas Capellanus, in Ovid's *Remedia Amoris* (a palinode to the *Ars Amatoria*) and Chaucer's own 'The Legend of Good Women'. 'The Parson's Tale' doesn't unsay the other Tales, let alone deny the value of fiction generally; it reinforces them, because it "says" in prose what stories in verse can't. Or to put it the other way round, it demonstrates the inevitability that poetic fiction will deviate from the norm, or present only a partial, subjective perspective on the normal moral landscape ∎

than most of the people in the other tales, not least in having achieved a sound, balanced marriage (and one oddly omitted from the marriage debate). As Derek Pearsall comments, "the fullest, most humanly realised, and on the whole happiest picture of marriage is that of Chauntecleer and Pertelote... It all speaks less of Chaucer's affection for birds (which, like Swift's for horses, was probably restrained) than of his disaffection for human beings."

But 'The Nun's Priest Tale' doesn't satirise human beings in general, so much as their restless seeking after some sort of authority to explain their world and to guide their behaviour. The comedy doesn't work as satire. It really functions as a kind of anti-masque, like those satyr plays that used to follow a trilogy of tragedies in the ancient Athenian theatre, or for that matter, like 'The Miller's Tale' following 'The Knight's Tale' with the same plot – two men pursuing the same young woman – but on the level of a parish squabble. 'The Miller's Tale' doesn't satirise the values taken so seriously in 'The Knight's Tale', but its low-life comedy blows it a raspberry, dispelling the tragic tension. It is, in fact, comic relief, in the true sense of that phrase.

Not till we get to 'The Parson's Tale' is authority cited seriously, in earnest, and for good motives; so Chaucer must have taken it seriously, and also our responsibility –difficult as it might be – to interpret it for ourselves. But 'The Parson's Tale' is prose and non-fiction. It was for imaginative scenarios to explore the comedy and pathos in the restless, often unstable, often anxious question of the nature of authority, how we should interpret it, and how we should live our lives by it.

The Knight's Tale

In Athens one May morning two prisoners of war, Palamon and Arcite, spy Emily, the beautiful younger sister of Queen Hippolyta, walking in the garden outside the window of their cell in Athens. Instantly both fall in love with her. The lady knows nothing of their interest, and in fact has determined not to marry anyone. In time Arcite is released from prison, but banished from the city on pain of death, only to return, disguised. Later Palamon too escapes, to hide near the city. One day the two men meet by chance in a wood, and immediately begin a fight to the death over Emily.

They are interrupted by Theseus, their lord and captor, his wife Hippolyta and Emily herself Theseus wants to execute the amorous young knights on the spot, but upon the women's pleas agrees instead to a formal tournament to be held in a year's time, with each knight accompanied by 100 others in his support.

In the great tournament Arcite defeats Palamon, but is later thrown off his horse, dying of his wounds. After a long period of mourning Theseus decrees that Palamon should marry Emily, and they live happily ever after.

Why is 'The Knight's Tale' so full of rhetoric?

Derek Pearsall argues that 'The Knight's Tale' was probably written well before many of the other *Canterbury Tales,* probably sometime between 'The Parliament of Fowls' and 'Troilus' – that is, in 1381-1382. "One function of *The Canterbury Tales,*" he adds, "was to provide a secure home for otherwise unattached compositions."

That might help explain why 'The Knight's Tale' is so different from the rest of *The Canterbury Tales.* For one thing, it's long. The story line is brief enough, yet the tale is the longest of all the tales in the collection, including that of the Parson. Why? In short, because the ratio of telling to showing is something like ten to one. And compared to the other tales, there is very little dramatic exchange between characters of the sort found in a play – even an ancient or classical play.

Far from being subtly disguised, the business of telling in 'The Knight's Tale' is foregrounded, right there on the surface. Take those explicit transitions for example: "And in this blisse lete I now Arcite./And speke I wol of Palamon a lite" (1449-1450), or "Now wol I turne to Arcite ageyn"

(1487-1488), not to mention "Now wol I... telle yow as pleynly as I kan/The grete effect, for which that I bygan" (2479-2482).

In *Chaucer and the French Tradition* (1957) Charles Muscatine has described this oft-noticed lack of drama in 'The Knight's Tale' in some detail. "The pace of the story is deliberately slow and majestic," he writes, and "there is an extraordinary amount of rhetorical *descriptio* in the poem, all of which slows the narrative". More to the point, much of this apparatus is "in excess to the demands of the story". Furthermore, there is "virtually no rapid dialogue. Speeches of twenty-five or thirty verses are normal... much in excess of what would be required in dramatic exchanges."

The Knight, followed by his son, the young Squire and a Yeoman
The Canterbury Tales, *mural by Ezra Winter, 1939*

35

For modern readers accustomed to narratives more direct in their exposition all this will require some acculturation. Take the rhetoric of 'The Knight's Tale', for a start – not just the abundant description, but other devices like the refusal from lines 2919 to 2964 to talk about Arcite's funeral ("shal nat be toold for me... Ne how... Ne how" and so forth), while elaborating every detail of the ceremony: what kinds of trees made up the pyre and how they were felled, how Emily fainted when she saw the construction, what spices and jewels were cast onto the fire, how the Greeks rode three times around it, and who wrestled best naked anointed with oil in the funeral games. All these and a myriad other details he "wol nat tellen".

Except that, of course, he does. This figure, often misnamed *occupatio*, not least by Chaucer scholars, is in fact *occultatio*, or *praeteritio*, commonly defined as a strategy of calling attention to a point by seeming to disregard it. Chaucer's use of it here is famously one of the longest and most elaborate in the literature.

All this runs up against a modern preference for plain speech, not to mention a suspicion of rhetoric as somehow false, if not downright deceitful, because it's so obviously artificial. But rhetoric is nothing more or less than the art of persuasion; the critical issue is, of what is it trying to persuade us, and how well does it manage it?

Again, a modern reader imbued with the

creative-writing-class aesthetic of 'show, don't tell'
will recoil from those lengthy emblematic accounts
of the gods' attributes inscribed on their oratories,
or in Saturn's reply to Venus's plea for help:

> *Myn is the drenchyng [drowning] in the see so*
> *wan [pale];*
> *Myn is the prison in the derke cote[cell],*
> *Myn is the stranglyng and hangyng by the throte,*
> *The murmure and the cherles [peasants]*
> *rebellyng,*
> *The groynynge [grumbling], and the pryvee*
> *[secret] empoysonyng;*
> *Myn is the ruyne of the hye halles,*
> *The fallynge of the toures and of the walles*
> *Upon the mynour [miner] or the carpenter,*
> *I slow [slew] Sampsoun, shakynge the piler;*
> *[piller] [2456-2466]*

"We can safely assume that Venus knows all about
her grandfather," comments Muscatine drily, so
"the long, self-descriptive introduction... must have
some function other than the dramatic". Exactly
so. On stage or in a novel Saturn's account of
himself would be redundant, but not in a late
medieval emblem. Saturn's attributes may not be
news to Venus, but they certainly are to the reader.
Instead of the god's more familiar associations
with sowing and the harvest, we get the darker
Saturn, the consort of Lua, the goddess of

destruction; Saturn who (via his association with the Greek god Cronus) killed his father and ate each of his children as they were born, in order to forestall the same fate.

Venus's own array of attributes, as set out in "portreyynge" on the walls of her oratory, also come as a surprise, disabusing the reader of any positive associations – say, with the exhilaration of love, or its power to redeem the ordinary. Instead we get the cold sighs and broken sleep (1920), "the firy strokes of the desirynge" (1922), "Charmes and Force, Lesynges [lies], Flaterye,/Despence [expense], Bisynesse, and Jalousye" (1926-1927), not to mention an eclectic catalogue of victims, like Hercules, Croesus and King Solomon, who for all their strength, wealth and wisdom, could not withstand love's onslaught.

Which is to say that these long emblematic passages pack a surprising force. Far from reiterating stock mythology, they come as news prompting thought. Far from presenting conventional wisdom through abstractions, they assault with concrete instances drawn from the extremes of human experience, and they come so fast and compressed as to leave the reader almost out of breath.

Why does Chaucer make his knights so similar?

The way to contextualise this over-explicitness of 'The Knight's Tale' is to recognise it as the most formal of all *The Canterbury Tales*, a fact not unconnected with its length. The poem is formal not only in rhetoric, but also in its general tone, in its plot structure, in its diction, and in its poetics. The formality of tone has a lot to do with the high sentence of the tale, as announced from the first line. "Whilom [once], as olde stories tellen us" (859) conveys the authority of tradition grounded in the classical past ('stories' means 'histories', not fiction), but the remainder of the tale, with its epic range of reference – involving both gods and humans in matters of high seriousness – and its quasi-tragic outcome, maintains this degree of solemnity throughout.

The formality of plot structure is something that Chaucer was at great pains to achieve when he shortened and shaped his chief source. Giovanni Boccaccio's neo-Virgilian epic, *La Teseide* (1340-1341), is around four times as long, including, for example, Theseus's subjugation of the Amazons and his capture of Hippolyta, their queen, matter deleted by Chaucer and summarised in just nine lines, from 875 to 884.

"Boccaccio is consistently attentive to the literal circumstances of his narrative," writes

Pearsall, "and his characters respond to events and each other in a natural and human way." Arcite declares his love to Emily, and she reciprocates, keeping his secret when he returns to Athens in disguise. As in Chaucer's version of the story, Arcite wins the tournament but is grievously wounded. As he dies he graciously bequeaths Emily to Palamon. So whereas the two knights are clearly distinguished in Boccaccio, "in Chaucer it is hard to tell them apart, and neither behaves well... It seems that Chaucer has deliberately levelled the two, so that the outcome of the story will appear not nobly tragic but bleakly capricious."

Chaucer imposes other symmetries on the Boccaccio tale too. Not only are the two knights of roughly equal moral stature, they each have a patron deity, to whom they pray in identical rhetorical format, described by Muscatine as "beginning with rhetorical *pronominatio* [addressing someone by their title or attributes] and continuing with a reference to the deity's relations with the opposite sex, a self-description by the speaker, a humble assertion of incompetence, a request for assistance and a promise to worship". Even the layout of the tournament is symmetrical: "The lists are circular in shape, a mile in circumference. They are entered from east and west by identical marble gates."

The poetics, too, contribute to the high seriousness of the tale. Among other sources,

Chaucer used figures and verse forms associated with two epic traditions: the Homeric and the Anglo-Saxon. The first provided the model of the extended simile, as when the pallor on the faces of Palamon and Arcite fighting in the wood is compared to that of the Thracian hunter standing in a clearing, armed with nothing but a spear against the lion and bear (1638-1649); or when Venus's fickle power over the hearts of lovers is compared to a Friday that starts sunny and ends raining "faste" (1534-1539).

The Anglo-Saxon epic – the eighth-century *Beowulf* is the prime example – offered a native poetics for the description of momentous events. Chaucer doesn't adopt – indeed, may not have been familiar with – the full rigours of the Anglo-Saxon line, with its four stresses divided by a caesura in the middle, but he did use the characteristic alliteration that linked the half lines across the divide, and he used the device for moments of crucial action. Here at last is the long anticipated tournament:

> *Ther shyveren shaftes upon sheeldes thikke.*
> *He [One] feeleth thurgh the herte-spoon*
> > *[breastbone] the prikke.*
> *Up spryngen speres twenty foot on highte;*
> *Out goon the swerdes in the silver brighte;*
> *The helmes they tohewen [hew] and to shrede*
> > *[shred]*

Out brest [bursts] the blood, with stierne
[powerful] stremes rede;
[2605-2610]*

There is even the ghost of an Old Norse *kenning* in that figurative compound, 'heart-spoon' for breastbone.

The obvious force of this formality of plot, diction and poetics is to generate a sense of order. "Order, which characterises the structure of the poem," writes Muscatine, "is also at the heart of its meaning." But what meaning? Muscatine is less clear on that point. 'The Knight's Tale' "is neither a story nor a static picture, but a sort of poetic pageant" of "those two noble activities, love and chivalry", and Theseus is their exemplar. Theseus, Muscatine claims, is "variously the ruler, the conqueror, the judge, and, not least, the man of pity ... the central figure in the poem's pattern of characters".

*Chaucer's use of alliteration for climactic moments in a romance of high seriousness was unusual in courtly poetry for a metropolitan audience, but it may have been part of that alliterative revival that began with the anonymous 'Wynnere and Wastoure' (c. 1352) and culminated in Langland's 'Piers Plowman' (1360 and later), and the work of the Pearl poet, 'Pearl' and 'Sir Gawain and the Green Knight' (both 1380).

What makes Theseus change his mind?

Order is certainly central to the thematics of the poem – but not as a given, universal value. Order is the subject of 'The Knight's Tale', a topic to be interrogated – its nature and limits to be explored – and not least in the figure of Theseus himself.

Theseus, Duke of Athens, has conquered Scythia, "the regne of Femenye" (866), where women called Amazons run the country and fight its wars. He marries the Queen of the Amazons thus re-imposing the proper hierarchy of gender, and brings her back to Athens, traditionally the seat of reason.

Just as they are about to enter the city they are met by a procession of Theban women, loudly lamenting, all "clad in clothes blake" (899). Theseus's first response is to accuse them of spoiling his happy homecoming "in greet envye/ Of myn honour" (907-908), but when he hears that Creon, Tyrant of Thebes, has forbidden their husbands either burial or cremation, he is moved to pity, and immediately declares war on Thebes, killing Creon in knightly combat and (incidentally) grievously wounding the Theban knights Arcite and Palamon along the way. Thus Theseus restores order in another theatre, reinstating proper funeral ritual.

Similarly, when Theseus and the ladies are out

hunting, they come upon Palamon and Arcite fighting in a wood, like wild animals – "a wood leon", "a crueel tigre", "wilde bores" (1656-1658). Chaucer shifts this setting from *La Teseide*, where the two knights first fight in Athens, in armour and following certain rules of the tournament, and it's clear that through the pun on 'wood' for 'forest' and 'mad'/'angry'/'wild', and the rhyme of 'wood' and 'blood' at the ends of lines 1659-1660, he wants to emphasise the lawlessness and irrationality of the fight.

So when Theseus, the man of reason and Duke of the city of reason, out hunting the "grete hert", with a pun linking the animal to the seat of emotions (1675), comes across the mayhem, the first thing he notices is that they are fighting "Withouten juge or oother officere" (1712), for

CHAUCER'S POLITICS

As a member of what we would now call the upper middle classes – that is, on the highest rank of society short of the aristocracy –

Chaucer had little time for the "voice of the people", especially after the Peasants' Revolt of 1381, when "Jakke Straw and his meynee", as Chaucer calls them in 'The Nun's Priest' Tale' (3394), swept into London, beheading the Lord Chancellor and the Archbishop of Canterbury, and burning down the palace of Chaucer's patron, John of Gaunt.

which breach of decorum they are to be executed forthwith. Until, that is, Hippolyta and Emily and "alle the ladyes in the compaignye" (1750) weep and fall on their knees for Theseus to have pity on these "gentil men... of greet estaat" (1753). And so he does, commuting the sentence to the controlled tournament to be held 50 weeks hence – but not before he has delivered a stinging satire on "The god of love, ah benedicite!... Now looketh, is nat that an heigh folye?/Who may been a fool but if [unless] he love?" (1795-1799).

"For pitee renneth soone in gentil herte" (1761) – well maybe soon, but not immediately. Theseus is not naturally or inherently "the man of pity", as Muscatine calls him. His first impulse is to bridle at the Theban women for spoiling his homecoming, and to kill the two knights discovered fighting in

---

Though Chaucer probably would not have gone as far as his fellow poet John Gower, whose 'Vox Clamantis' calls the Peasants' Revolt the work of the Antichrist, "his view of the common people", as Derek Pearsall has put it, was "one of routine contempt for them en masse, as in the apostrophe against the 'stormy peple, Unsad [inconstant] and evere untrewe' of The Clerk's Tale (IV, 995-1001), and routine admiration for them in their individual roles of humble and patient obligation, like the Plowman of The General Prologue".

If Chaucer had a positive political philosophy, it was his belief in "commune profit", that is, the good of the commonwealth as a whole. This ideal had the attraction, as Pearsall

the wood. When the wounded bodies of Palamon and Arcite are brought to him from under the heap of corpses following the Theban-Athenian war, his first reaction is to sentence them both to prison perpetually, without ransom. Later when Arcite's friend Protheus begs him to let Arcite go, Theseus agrees to free him, unransomed, providing he never again shows his face in any country governed by Theseus, on pain of having his head struck from his shoulders. Later, of course, the disguised Arcite serves with such distinction in Athens that Theseus makes him his squire.

In other words, there is always an element of debate between Theseus's first reaction to an event and his second thoughts. More often than not his initial harsh judgement is tempered by a woman, or several women. Again, this role of women as

remarks, of being "inherently admirable and at the same time satisfactorily unspecific".

As part of his class outlook, Chaucer was also against inherited privilege, as his little moral ballad 'Gentilesse' makes clear:

Vyce [vice] may wel be heir to old richesse,

But ther may no man, as men may wel see,

Bequethe his heir his virtuous noblesse

(That is appropred unto no degree ...)

In expanded form this is the lesson the old hag teaches the rapist knight in 'The Wife of Bath's Tale' and, as Pearsall says, it "is one in which Chaucer's imaginative powers are fully engaged, and one in which he may therefore be more fully alive" to its political and social implications ∎

mediator is a Chaucerian innovation. In *La Teseide* (Book V, verses 84-88), when Teseo, hunting with Emily, surprises the two love rivals fighting – not as animals in a wood but as proper knights, kitted out in armour and following the rules of tournament combat – he at first feels contempt* when they reveal who they are, but then thanks them for being so honest. When they reveal the cause of their combat, he is deeply moved and pardons them. No woman intercedes.

What all this seems to be suggesting is that real order – humane order, order that works – is some kind of synthesis between the manly head and the womanly heart. Theseus may have imposed the conventional male dominance over the "regne of Femenye", but it takes femininity to set his judgements straight. As Jill Mann puts it in *Feminizing Chaucer*, "The 'compassioun' Theseus feels for women is itself a womanly quality implanted in him. It feminises him without rendering him effeminate." And Mann is surely right to claim that "Theseus's constant refashioning of his plans is... a sign of strength rather than a betrayal of weakness". This extra dimension to Chaucer's version of the hero may also be a clue to what is, philosophically speaking, the tale's biggest departure from *La Teseide*, Theseus's great concluding speech on "The

*The verb is 'sdegnò' in Boccaccio, literally 'disdained'.

Firste Moevere of the cause above" (2987).

From line 3017 Chaucer paraphrases fairly closely the Boccaccio thesis that since everything dies, we that live still should make virtue of necessity:

E pero far della necessitate
Virtù quando bisogna è sapienza.
Ed il contrario è vanitate...
(*La Teseide* XII, 11)*

Coming after Boccaccio's gloomy vision of all nature eventually wearing away – even oaks and stones – this sentiment comes as cold, stoic comfort, or a sort of shrugging of the shoulders, like the Second Lord's "Let's make the best of it" at the end of Shakespeare's *Coriolanus*. This impression is strengthened when you recall that the Italian "virtù" is much closer to "manly courage" than to the English meaning of "moral good".

But Chaucer's "firste moevere" part of the speech, drawing on his own translation of Boethius's *The Consolation of Philosophy*,** contextualises Boccaccio's pessimism within wider providential order motivating the

*And so it's wise to make a virtue of necessity, when you have to, and to do otherwise is vanity.

**Boece, Book II, Metrum 8; Book III, Metrum 9; Book IV, Prosa 6, Metrum 7.

universe, binding the four elements of fire, air, water and earth, together with all animate and inanimate creation that they make up, with a "faire cheyne of love". So although Boccaccio's oaks and stones may in time wear away, by "progressiouns", in Chaucer they will "enduren by successiouns" (3013-3014) – that is, be renewed in the logic of a larger natural process.

It's all a matter perspective. From the vantage point of the mutable world – Teseo's in *La Teseide*, for instance – all life, subject to fortune, tends eventually to decay. It is from this viewpoint too that the two lovers bemoan the ironies of their fate, one being close to Emily but locked in prison, the other having been set free but banished from Athens. The First Mover, however, sees with providence – "purveyaunce", foresight – which embraces and encompasses the narrower arena of fortune.

Yet even this enlarged view of the cosmos remains a pagan one. Love is not redemptive here, as the pictures on the walls of Venus's oratory make clear. Mankind is not redeemed from the Fall by the sacrifice of Christ, and there is no hint of a Christian salvation for Arcite. When Arcite dies in *La Teseide*, his spirit flies up to the eighth sphere, the realm of the fixed stars. From here he looks back upon the earth, judging it to be worthless by comparison with heaven (XI, 1-2).

But Chaucer was not willing to allow Arcite

even that limited degree of afterlife, although he does use this ending for Troilus at the end of 'Troilus and Criseyde'. Instead he has the Knight dismiss the question:

> *His spirit chaunged hous and wente ther,*
> *As I cam nevere, I kan nat tellen wher.*
> *Therfore I stynte [stop]; I nam no divinistre;*
> *[theologian]*
> *Of soules fynde I nat in this registre*
> *[2809-2812]*

Muscatine writes of Chaucer's "lightness" over the death of Arcite, with no real tragedy and no moral lesson drawn. Pearsall comments on the instability of tone in serious passages such as the descriptions of Arcite's death (2759-2760), and of the fate of his soul (2809-2816). "It might appear that Chaucer has not yet mastered the techniques of narrative control," he adds.

These are serious misjudgements. There is nothing facetious about this deliberate alteration to the Boccaccian model, and Chaucer is quite in control. This is, after all, the Knight, that Christian crusader, speaking to other Christians on their way to Canterbury. Toward the end of his tale he is drawing the line of demarcation between the pagan world view and the Christian, implying, as it were, that for all its chivalry and high sentence, for all its enlightened philosophical inquiry into the human predicament, the classical world with its gods, heroes and lovers was in the end a glorious spectacle, an entertainment, rather than the everyday reality of the Christian pilgrim.

The Miller's and The Reeve's Tales

'The Miller's Tale'

In 'The Miller's Tale' an old carpenter called John is newly married to Alisoun, a beautiful 18-year-old. They live in Oxford, where they have taken in a boarder, a student by the name of Nicholas. One day when John is absent Nicholas makes a grab for Alisoun and declares his passion for her. She refuses at first, but eventually agrees to sleep with him if they can get her jealous husband out of the way. Nicholas, supposedly learned in astrology, convinces John that next Monday night at nine it will rain so heavily that within an hour the whole world will be drowned. Their only hope is to find kneading troughs for each of them to sleep in, rig them to hang from the roof, then cut them free to float away on the flood. John agrees.

Meanwhile, Alisoun has another lover in Absolon, the fastidious parish clerk, who moons about outside her ground-floor window on the very Monday night in question. She rejects him, but when he asks for a kiss at least, she puts her rear end out of the window. When he realises what's happened, the furious Absolon goes to a blacksmith and comes back with a red-hot ploughshare. Nicholas, thinking to improve the joke by getting Absolon to kiss his arse in turn, gets branded, screams with pain and calls out for water. Hearing that last word, John wakes, and assuming the flood is upon them, cuts the ropes securing his tub to the rafters, and falls to the floor, breaking his arm. When the neighbours call in the next morning, they mock him for a cuckold, and a crazy one at that.

'The Reeve's Tale'

'The Reeve's Tale' concerns a cheating miller called Simkin and two Cambridge students, John and Aleyn, determined to catch him out. They bring him a large sack of wheat to mill, asking if they can watch Simkin grind it, pretending interest in the milling process, but really to make sure he doesn't keep some of the flour for himself. Simkin is on to their ruse, however, and causes a distraction by un-tethering their horse. While they chase it, the miller steals half a bushel of the students' flour, giving it to his wife with which to bake a cake.

By the time the young men retrieve their horse, it's too late to set off for the college, so they negotiate the price of an overnight stay with the miller and his family. There are only three beds in one bedroom, so Simkin and his wife will sleep in one, their 20-year-old daughter Malyne in the second, while the students will share the third. A six-month-old baby sleeps in a cradle at the foot of the miller's bed.

After a night of heavy drinking the miller's family fall dead asleep, while John and Aleyn plot their revenge. Aleyn gets into Malyne's bed and has at her almost before she wakes. While Simkin's wife visits the privy, John moves the baby's cradle to the foot of his own bed, which the wife, feeling for the crib in the dark, mistakes for her own. As she slips into the bed, John slips into her.

As they awake next morning, Malyne, now in love with him, tells Aleyn where to find the loaf made of the purloined flour. On getting up, Aleyn goes to the bed he assumes is John's, because lacking a cradle at its foot, shakes Simkin awake and boasts that he has "thries [thrice] in this shorte nyght/Swyved [fucked] the milleres doghter bolt upright" (4265-4266). Enraged, Simkin wakes his wife, who, mistaking her husband for one of the students, sets about him with a club. In the uproar John and Aleyn make their escape with the cake, without paying for their overnight stay.

Why do these two stories follow 'The Knight's Tale'?

These two tales follow 'The Knight's Tale', but they do little to uphold the Knight's dignified tone of high seriousness. 'The Miller's Tale' and 'The Reeve's Tale' are fabliaux. Other fabliaux in *The Canterbury Tales* include 'The Shipman's Tale' and 'The Summoner's Tale'. 'The Merchant's Tale' also embodies aspects of the genre.

The Riverside Chaucer describes a fabliau as "a brief comic tale in verse, usually scurrilous and often scatological or obscene". Typically, the story is set in the present, and involves characters drawn from ordinary life, like millers, carpenters, priests, students and what *The Riverside Chaucer* calls "restless wives". But in case that brief definition leads to the conclusion that fabliaux were really novels before their time, there are three points of difference from modern fiction to bear in mind.

First, however many concrete details they draw from contemporary life, fabliaux are not 'realistic' in the same way as novels are. In what realistic novel, let alone in real life, would you find people so gullible as Simkin and old John? Or two students (however clever) as ingenious and sexually adventurous as Aleyn and John – or for that matter, sex so quick, easy and mechanical as in that miller's overpopulated bedroom?

In the fabliau nearly every event, nearly every

detail of setting and every stock character, from jealous husband, over-watched wife and lusty student, is there to serve the tale's climactic ending. Why does Nicholas, who lives in the Miller's house anyway, need such an elaborate ruse to sleep with his wife? Why is the cradle – presumably a heavy wooden one – in 'The Reeve's Tale' so portable and the room so dark that only by feeling for it can the characters tell where they are? Why is Absolon said to be somewhat squeamish of farting and bad language (3337-3338)? Why does the hinged window in the carpenter's house only come up to Absolon's breast (3695-3696)? And so on.

Second, the morality of the fabliau is not that of the novel, in which the protagonists' advance in intellectual and emotional experience is linked to their moral progress. As the editors of *The Riverside Chaucer* put it, "'fabliau justice' does not always coincide with conventional morality: greed, hypocrisy, pride are invariably punished, but so too are old age, mere slow-wittedness, and, most frequently, the presumption of a husband... who attempts to guard his wife's chastity". Putting the issue more positively, V. A. Kolve suggests that the abundant natural imagery in 'The Miller's Tale' invokes "a whole, and wholly attractive, category of life lived outside of morality... an animal world in which instinct takes the place that reason holds for man, a world in which instinct and necessity are one".

The Reeve (far left) leaving the gates of Southwark with Chaucer, the Clerk of Oxenford and the Cook. Engraving by William Blake, 1810

Third, although the Miller and the Reeve are both "cherles" – rude, unlettered men – who tell tales of "harlotrie", as Chaucer the pilgrim admits in 'The Miller's Prologue' (1382, 1384), their tales were really written by a learned diplomat and civil servant for a bourgeois readership. And although versions of these stories about switched cradles, Noah's flood, and what Chaucer critics delicately refer to as the "misdirected kiss" had been passed around by word of churlish mouth for centuries, they had also been turned into literature by authors of romance. For example, there is a version of 'The Reeve's Tale' in Jean Bodel's 'Gombert et les Deux Clers' (1200) and another in Boccaccio's *Il*

The Miller, in the lead, piping the band out of Southwark.
The Canterbury Tales, *mural by Ezra Winter, 1939*

Decamerone, Day 9, story 6. Other stories in *Il Decamerone* also contain fragments of these orally transmitted jokes.

So much for fabliau in general. What about these two? Well the first and most obvious thing to note is that 'The Reeve's Tale' is shorter and more sparing in detail than 'The Miller's Tale'. Apart from the northern dialect spoken by the students – admirably noted in *The Riverside Chaucer* text – there isn't much there that isn't needed to set up the joke.

A small part of that joke is the tale's parodic inversion of the traditional inventory by which the beauty of the lady is anatomised in courtly love romance. Conventionally, the lady had fair hair, blue eyes, fine eyebrows, small breasts, a slender waist, small feet, and wore clothes embroidered in gold. Malyne, by contrast is a "wenche thikke and wel ygrowen", with a pug nose, "buttokes brode and brestes rounde and hye" (3973-3974). But at least her hair was "right fair", as the Reeve adds grudgingly.

Compared to 'The Reeve's Tale', 'The Miller's Tale' is much fuller of naturalistic detail, a "fabliau at the stage of richest elaboration", as Charles Muscatine has put it. "In no other naturalistic poem of Chaucer is practical circumstance so clearly tended, and practical detail so closely accounted for." So we get the name not just of the town it takes place in, but of neighbouring towns also. Almost all the characters are named. There is a "scrupulous accounting of the days of the week and of the hours of the crucial day".

But how do these two examples of the genre function in the larger context of *The Canterbury Tales*? We know they belong together in this order because they are part of 'Fragment I', which includes 'The General Prologue' and 'The Knight's Tale'. These so-called fragments are not pieces of manuscript, but, to quote *The Riverside Chaucer*, "editorial units determined by the existence of internal signs of linkage – bits of conversation or narrative that explicitly refer to a tale just told or to one that immediately follows".

At first sight these "bits of conversation" – the pilgrims' pungent comments on (or arguments following) stories just told, expressions of support or disapproval of other pilgrims' demeanour or opinions – are there mainly to add realism to the framing narrative. Yet the rough dialogue sometimes amounts to more than local colour So when in 'The Miller's Prologue' the host disputes whether the Miller is sober enough to tell a tale of his own, his loud persistence allows Chaucer the narrator-pilgrim to absolve himself from the opprobrium of writing a bawdy tale. Don't blame me, he says; I'm just reporting what happened. Those who are offended can turn the page and choose another story. And don't take the joke too seriously (3171-3186).

And there is a theme running through the interstices between the three tales of Fragment I. When the Knight finishes speaking, the Host asks the Monk if he can tell "'Somewhat to quite with the Knyghtes tale'" (3119). When the Miller drunkenly pushes himself forward, he boasts:

> 'I kan [know] a noble tale for the nones
> [occasion],
> With which I wol now quite the Knyghtes tale.'
> [3126-3127]

And when the Miller finishes his tale, most of the company laugh and joke about the fate of "Absolon

and hende Nicholas". Not the Reeve, though.
"By cause he was of carpenteris craft" (3861),
he suggests to the Miller that "'ful wel koude I
thee quite'" (3864) for his humiliation of John
the carpenter.

Is Chaucer parodying the conventions of courtly love?

The verb 'quite' had several meanings in the mid to
late 14th century. In the Host's usage, it suggests
"to equal". The Miller means "to repay", as of a
debt. The Reeve's sense of the word is more "to pay
back", as in to get even. The Reeve's revenge seems

limited to portraying a miller equally gullible as carpenter John, and much less pleasant: thieving and violent. "Thus have I quyt the Millere in my tale," as he boasts in the last line.

The Miller's address to 'The Knight's Tale' is a good deal more complex, not least because he takes the assault on courtly love romance much further than does the Reeve. As we have seen , he parodies the Knight's beginning and ending. Following the same sonorous "Whilom" (used in both cases), the "duc that highte [was called] Theseus" becomes a "riche gnof [lout] that gestes heeld to bord". Concluding a romance of two noble kinsmen in courtly pursuit of a princess, the

document. The tales told on the way to Canterbury all pretend to be 'oral', but exist within a frame narrative "explicitly addressed to the private reader" (Pearsall again). A clue that the tales were meant to be read comes in the Miller's advice to "Turne over the leef and chese another tale" if you object to his story's profanity. "Chaucer had no copy of *The Canterbury Tales* made, and did not prepare the work for publication," Pearsall says. "Parts of it circulated in written copies, but it was not until after his death that the work began to be copied as a whole." All this came well before the invention of printing, of course. Even so, by the end of the 15th century Chaucer had been elevated to the status of the "aurerate laureate" by the poets John Lydgate and Thomas Hoccleve, and the influential scribe John Shirley. This "social and collaborative nature of literary production", as Seth Lehrer calls it in his *Chaucer and his Readers*, gave Chaucer's work a high reputation ∎

Knight signs off with "And God save al this faire compaignye! Amen" (3108). The Miller, after replicating the love triangle on the level of village farce, ends with: "This tale is doon, and God save al the rowte!" (3854).

The Miller has a lot of fun with promoting Absolon's pretentions to be a courtly lover himself. As Muscatine points out, the conventional courtly lover "'rometh' perhaps, but he does not 'swelte and swete' nor does he catch up on his sleep before a sleepless night" (3694, 3703, 3685). And though the lover may "hym arraieth gay, at poynt-devys", we're unlikely to descend to the detail of him sweetening his breath with "greyn and lycorys" (3689-3690). "The courtly delicacy of speech and of toilette" – Muscatine again – "have become in this smalltown, provincial version the anal-retentive, squeamish spotlessness... punished with terrible aptness at the end."

Indeed, the comic clash of styles is replicated in the ironic couplet rhyming "devys'/'lycorys". And there are others like it. Absolon, paying romantic court to Alisoun, claims (quite conventionally) to be so in love with her as to have lost his appetite:

> *"I may nat ete na moore than a mayde."*
> *'Go fro the wyndow, Jakke fool,' she sayde;*
> *[3707-3708]*

And after kissing her arse:

> *And seyde. "Fy! allas! what have I do?"*
> *'Tehee!' quod she, and clapte the wyndow to,*
>
> *[3739-3740]*

And when he returns with the hot iron, bent on revenge:

> *"Spek, sweete bryd [bird], I noot nat where thou*
> *art."*
>
> *This Nicholas anon leet fle a fart,*
>
> *[3805-3806]*

But when it comes to his inventory of the lady's beauty, 'The Miller's Tale', in keeping with its richer store of naturalistic detail, goes well beyond a simple parody of the courtly style. Alisoun certainly differs from the conventional lady – her eyebrows plucked and "blake as any sloo", her smock, not gown, embroidered with black silk rather than gold – but she has a natural beauty not shared by the ill-favoured Malyne, one reinforced by the abundance of wholesome natural images to flesh out her portrait: the "per-jonette tree", the "wolle... of a wether [wool... sheep]", the "swalwe", the "joly colt" (3246, 3248, 3249, 3258, 3263).

So the conventions of the courtly love romance are not simply mocked here; they are supplanted by a new set of rules, what V. A. Kolve calls "an animal world in which instinct takes the place that reason holds for man".

Which brings us back to that theme of "quiting". Another contemporary meaning of the word – indeed the first listed in the Oxford English Dictionary – is "to set free", "to release", much as in modern "acquit". Granted the Reeve wants to "quite" the Miller in the sense of pay him back, and the Miller want to repay the Knight, but might there be a sense too in which the Miller's tale works to set free 'The Knight's Tale'? This is as much to say that 'The Miller's Tale' acts as an antimasque to 'The Knight's Tale', relieving its tension as did a satyr play following a trilogy of Athenian tragedies. But it also works to release the reader from the oppressive tragedy of Arcite's death, and the heavy burden of Theseus's moralising about the cosmic order.

The Wife of Bath

In her long and lively Prologue the Wife of Bath satirises the lazy-minded misogyny that derives |its spurious authority from the classics, then sets out to challenge traditional teaching on marriage in the Gospels that interprets the relationship allegorically as spiritual rather than literally as physical, emotional and social. Her tale illustrates exactly the opposite, though, because it is about a violent and snobbish knight forced to accept that a woman's beauty lies not on the surface but in the moral worth of her character.

Is the Wife of Bath just a widow on the make?

The Wife of Bath, married five times, with her spurs, her fine red stockings and her hat the size of a shield – is she a grotesque figure or does she stand for another of those 'estates' represented by the other pilgrims on their way to Canterbury? In *Chaucer and the Subject of History* Lee Patterson calls her a "typical widow on the make". Derek Pearsall in his *Life of Geoffrey Chaucer* points to the "increasing participation of women in the economy... partly due to post-Black Death labour shortages", and suggests that as a married woman she "could have the status of a *femme sole*, that is, one who would be allowed to trade as if she were single and to make contracts in her own name". So maybe she plays a traditional social role.

When it comes to religion, though, the Wife is far from typical. As Alastair Minnis reminds us in *Fallible Authors*, the orthodox view persisted that women could not be teachers or preachers, and certainly not interpreters of scripture. Indeed, in his own prologue immediately following her tale, the Friar gently rebukes her, suggesting that women should stick to entertaining subjects and leave Biblical interpretation to (male) preachers and scholars (1275-1277).

The Wife's contempt for conventional Biblical exegesis is easy enough to understand: so much of it has been deployed against women. Her fifth husband, Jankyn, the jolly scholar who was so good in bed, was forever reading to her out of a big book full of misogynistic sentiments drawn from the classics, like Theophrastus's fourth century BC *Liber aureolus de nuptiis* (Golden Book on Marriage) and St Jerome's *Epistola adversus Jovinianum* (Letter Against Jovinian) (ca 393 AD) – to the point where, tried beyond all patience, she tore a sheet out of it, thus provoking a mighty row between them.

Theophrastus, successor to Aristotle and head of the Peripatetic school of philosophy in Athens, was a distinguished metaphysician, logician and botanist. On marriage, however, he took a less than logical line: he was against it. St Jerome was equally belligerent. Jovinian opined that a virgin is no better than a wife in the sight of God, for which St Jerome attacked him bitterly.*

The Wife confronts these supposedly learned assaults on women by repeatedly and sarcastically reiterating the various charges as though hardly deserving of a serious response. This happens in all those passages beginning with "Thou seist" or

*Excerpts from *Theophrastus* and *Against Jovinian*, together with Walter Map, *The Letter of Valerius to Ruffinus against Marriage* (another misogynist text bound in Jankyn's book) can be found in V.A. Kolve and Glending Olson, eds., Geoffrey Chaucer, *The Canterbury Tales: Fifteen Tales and the General Prologue*. New York: Norton Critical Editions, 2005 (henceforth NCE), 357-80.

"Thou seydest". "Thou" is not a specific person, but a hypothetical old dotard (235) or old lecher (242) – that is, a straw man supposedly laying down the anti-feminist line. Hence:

> *Thow seyst that droppyng [dripping, leaking]*
> > *houses and eek smoke,*
> *And chidyng wyves maken men to flee*
> *Out of hir owene houses; ah benedicitee!*
> *What eyleth [ails] swich an old man for to chide!*
> > *[278-281]*

This repeats a jibe in St Jerome, but doesn't really repudiate it with a counter-assertion, settling instead for an ad hominem attack on the accuser – playing the man not the ball, as they say in football. But as Barrie Ruth Straus points out in her essay "The Subversive Discourse of the Wife of Bath", by accusing the men of chiding, which she does also in lines 242, 244 and 262, the Wife turns the tables on men, reversing their stereotype of the chiding wife.

In *Chaucer's Sexual Poetics* (1989), Carolyn Dinshaw writes that the Wife's tactic of repeating the anti-feminist line of attack strengthens her argument: "Rather than embodying what patriarchal discourse *can't* say, she is enacting precisely what patriarchal discourse *does* say, and says endlessly in [its] univocal chant." In other words, in her mimicry "she not only uncovers what is hidden in the workings of patriarchal ideology, but simultaneously appropriates the place of the Other that ideology openly creates".

How subversive is the Wife of Bath?

The only trouble with this line of critical reading, however, is that from another standpoint, the tactic weakens her case: in denouncing the anti-feminist sentiments (and not all that conclusively – more in 'yah-boo' mode), she is moved to reiterate them; so they become part of her speech; 'their' voice colonises hers. To adopt the Foucauldian evaluation embraced by David Aers in his *Chaucer, Langland and the Creative Imagination*, this process of mimicry perpetuates the outlook against which she rails. Even Dinshaw has to admit that the Wife willingly embraces the patriarchal commodification of sexual relations when she admits "al is for to selle" (414).

Where the Wife really challenges traditional wisdom, therefore, is when – instead of repeating the charges against women – she refuses to engage with them at all. Because Christ went to only the one wedding at Cana, does that mean she should have taken no further husbands after the first one died? And why did Christ reprove the Samaritan woman at the well for her five husbands? "What that he mente therby I kan

Opposite: The Wife of Bath (centre), engraving by William Blake, 1810

TEN FACTS ABOUT
THE CANTERBURY TALES

1.

Chaucer's original plan for *The Canterbury Tales* was for each pilgrim to tell four stories – two on the way to Canterbury and two on the trip back to London. Since there are 34 pilgrims, this would have made 136 tales in all. In the event there are only 24. It's not known whether Chaucer changed his mind about the total or left the plan incomplete at his death in 1400.

2.

The Tales' narrators, though characterised (often caricatured) in 'The General Prologue', invariably tell their tales from an omniscient point of view. That is, they possess a god-like knowledge of all places, people and events in their stories, including the thoughts of all the characters.

3.

First printed in 1476, 76 years after Chaucer's death, William Caxton's volume of *The Canterbury Tales* was the first book in English to be printed in England. It has never been out of print since. The only copy of this first edition still in private hands fetched £4,621,500 at auction in 1998, making it the most expensive book sold until 2013.

4.

The pilgrims never actually reach Canterbury. The last offering, 'The Parson's Tale', is told on the outskirts of the City, and the framing narrative has nothing to say about the trip back to London.

5.

Chaucer's Monk, that "lord ful fat" who sidestepped St. Augustine's austere monastic rule in order to overeat and go hunting, was no more an invention of satire than Robin Hood's portly Friar Tuck was of folklore. A 2004 study by archaeologists at University College London found that medieval monks really were gluttons. Analysis of skeletons from Tower Hill, Bermondsey, and Merton abbeys showed widespread signs of arthritis in knees, hips and fingertips, indicating that the monks were seriously obese. Suet, lard and butter were wolfed down in "startling quantities", the study found. According to Philippa Patrick, of the Institute of Archaeology, "They were taking in about 6,000 calories a day, and 4,500 even when they were fasting."

6.

Chaucer was the first poet to be buried in Westminster Abbey – not because of his literary output but because he had been Clerk of Works to the Palace of Westminster.

7.

The iconoclastic Terry Jones has written two books on Chaucer. In *Chaucer's Knight* (1980) he argued that far from being a Christian crusader who "loved chivalrie,/Trouthe and honour, fredom and courtesie", the Knight was a cold-blooded mercenary. In *Who Murdered Chaucer?* (2003) he accused that great scourge of the Lollards, Thomas Arundel, Archbishop of Canterbury, of arranging the poet's death in revenge for his satirical portraits of churchmen.

8.

In 1380, when Chaucer was 39, married, with one son and another on the way, a certain Cecilia Chaumpaigne signed a deed agreeing to release him "all manner of actions such as they relate to my rape or any other thing or cause". In return, Chaucer acknowledged and paid a debt of £10, the equivalent of £129,000 in today's money, and roughly half of his current annual income.

9.

Chaucer's only surviving non-fictional autobiographical statement – and that only reported in indirect speech – is his evidence given as a witness in a case before the Court of Chivalry to decide which family, the Scropes or the Grosvenors, had the right to bear the arms of a blue shield with a diagonal gold stripe down it.

Chaucer testified that Sir Richard Scrope had indeed fought in France under the said insignia. Asked whether he had ever heard that Sir Robert Grosvenor had challenged the Scrope's right to the arms, Chaucer said "no, but that he was once in Friday Street, London, and walking through the street, he observed a new sign hanging out with these arms thereon, and inquired 'what inn that was that had hung out these arms of Scrope?' And one answered him, saying, 'They are not hung out, Sir, for the arms of Scrope, nor painted there for those arms, but they are painted and put there by a Knight of the county of Chester, called Sir Robert Grosvenor;' and that was the first time that he ever heard speak of Sir Robert Grosvenor, or his ancestors, or of any one bearing the name of Grosvenor."

10.

The Canterbury Tales contains literally hundreds of still-current English words first used in a work of literature. 'The General Prologue' alone accounts for 48 from 'alight' and 'bagpipe' to 'stew', 'wallet' and 'whistling'. 'The Miller's Tale' contributes 24 words, including 'chant', 'haunch-bone' and (inescapably) 'fart'. From 'The Wife of Bath's Tale' we get 23, running from 'annex' to 'vacation'. 'The Knight's Tale' is more Latinate and less cheerful in many of its 70, of which 'execute', 'funeral', 'melancholic' and 'menacing' are typical.

nat seyn" (70).

It is on the institution of marriage that the Wife of Bath is truly subversive. The standard teaching on Christian marriage is based on St Paul's letters to the Corinthians and the Ephesians. It is also set out in 'The Parson's Tale', X, 915- 943. Paul teaches that the highest calling is virginity, but that for those who cannot abstain from sexual relations, "let them marry, for it is better to marry than to be burnt" (I Corinthians 7, 8-9). Marriage is a divinely sanctioned figure of the union between Christ and the Church. "Therefore as the Church is subject to Christ, so also let the wives be to their husbands in all things." But if wives have to obey their husbands, "So also ought men to love their wives as their own bodies. He that loveth his wife, loveth himself" (Ephesians 5, 24, 28).* Over and against the Wife's tactical bewilderment about the wedding at Cana, the standard interpretation would follow through the four levels of allegory, as understood by medieval Biblical exegesis: the literal, the allegorical (or typological), the moral (or tropological) and the anagogical (eschatological, or leading to salvation).

On the literal level, the wedding at Cana in Galilee goes as the story reads in John 2, 1-11. Jesus is invited to the wedding, along with his

*This is from the Douy/Reims translation of the Latin Vulgate, the Bible that Chaucer knew and used.

mother and disciples. When his mother tells him that the wine has run out, Jesus says, "Woman, what have I to do with you? My time has not yet come." But he goes to the pantry, where there are six stone pots, and suggests to the waiters that they fill the pots to the brim with water, then draw from them and take the result to the steward. When he tastes, the steward calls to the bridegroom to compliment him on keeping the best wine till last, when the worst was usually served because by then the guests were too drunk to notice the difference. This was Christ's first miracle.

On the allegorical level the six stone jars represent the six ages of the world – the first five as recorded in the Old Testament* and the sixth, Christ's time, in which He comes to redeem the world. The water signifies the flesh, the wine the spirit. On the moral level, the marriage taking place is between God and the soul. The transformation from water to wine signifies the need for the spiritual dimension of internal devotion. Finally, the anagogical meaning is that through Christ, God leads us from the world of the flesh through the world of the spirit to our ultimate salvation.

*The idea is developed by St Augustine in his De catechizandis rudibus (On the catechizing of the uninstructed). The first age runs from the creation to Noah; the second from Noah to Abraham; the third from Abraham to King David; the fourth from David to the Babylonian captivity; the fifth from the captivity to the advent of Jesus Christ.

As for "what that [Christ] mente" by His
exchange with the Samaritan woman, this too
was interpreted as the crucial moment when
the spirit fulfilled the letter of the law. On the
literal level, as the story reads in John, 4, 5-26,
a Samaritan woman is drawing water from a well;
Jesus, arriving at the sixth hour, sits on the well
and asks her for some. She asks why a Jew should
ask a Samaritan for water. He replies that if she
knew who he was, she wouldn't ask that, but would

The Prioress; the Nun; and three priests, The Canterbury Tales, mural by Ezra Winter

instead have asked for living water. For "whoever
drinks the water of this well will thirst again, but
whoever drinks the living water that I give, will
never thirst again". She asks for it. He replies,
"go call your husband". She says: "Sir, I have no
husband." He replies, that's right, "you have had
five husbands, but the man with whom you are
living now is not your husband". She answers:
"Sir, I see you are a prophet."

On the allegorical level, the Samaritan woman

represents either the Jews of the Synagogue or the pagan church of the gentiles. The five husbands are the five ages of the Old Testament. The water of the well is the religion of the letter, while the water offered by Christ is the religion of the spirit. The sixth husband is Christ himself, who, coming at the sixth hour, represents the beginning of the sixth age, the age of the gospel.

On the moral level the Samaritan woman is the inferior part of the reason. The five husbands are the five senses, to which the Samaritan woman gave herself in youth, so that they ruled her like husbands. The sixth husband is spiritual understanding.

On the anagogical level, the whole passage was read as God's guiding us from a fallen world,

RELIGION AND THE CANTERBURY TALES

It is difficult for the post-reformation – not to mention the secular – imagination to comprehend the spread and grip of the church in Chaucer's place and time.

There were more churches in London than in any other city in Europe, according to Peter Ackroyd in his *London: The Biography.* "Beside the 126 parish churches there were sixteen covenantal churches...seven great friaries...five priories...four large nunneries and five priests' colleges...Of the hospitals and refuges for the

via spiritual understanding, to Paradise.

So the Wife either doesn't know these hidden meanings, or does know them, but pretends not to because they don't suit her argument; besides, she disdains "glossing up and down". In any case, to quote D. W. Robertson Jr.'s *A Preface to Chaucer*:

> When the wife denies the argument that Christ's attendance at one wedding was an indication that a person should marry only once, she not only implies that she denies the sacrament or spirit of marriage, but also indicates a preference on her own part for the laws of the first five ages, for the 'oldness of the letter', for the insipid water of pleasure rather than the wine of spiritual inebriation.

sick and indigent we have records of seventeen...This is not to mention the chantries, the church schools and the private chapels."

The church was the biggest landlord and employer inside and outside the city walls, says Ackroyd. "Many thousands of people, both secular and spiritual, owed their livings to the great abbeys and monastic foundations of the city."

So it's no wonder that so many of Chaucer's characters in *The Canterbury Tales*, like the Friar, Pardoner, Prioress, Monk, Parson and others, are either employed by the Church, or victimised by it, like the poor old widows in 'The Friar's Tale' – or, like the Wife of Bath, in dispute with it. It's also why they can't get it out of their everyday discourse: "for Christes passion"/ "by him that harwed helle!"/ "By my savacioun"/ "For Christes swete tree!" Oaths, however

"Thus what the Wife of Bath fails to understand," Robertson continues, "is the spiritual significance of Christ's words to the Samaritan, just as she has failed to understand the spiritual significance of marriage. Like the Samaritan, she prefers the Old Law to the New, or the law of fallen nature to the law of grace." Robertson also takes the Wife to task for quoting St Paul out of context, a process that supports "superficially credible arguments which may easily entrap the unwary".

But just who are these "unwary"? Surely not the other pilgrims or Chaucer's contemporary readers, for whom these standard interpretations would have been familiar through sermons and wedding services. Even Robertson admits: "These are not obscure ideas. Pilgrims to Canterbury would have

disparaged by the Pardoner at his most vehemently hypocritical, are inextricable from the common vernacular of *The Canterbury Tales*.

"Six of the longest and most detailed portraits in 'The General Prologue' are devoted to ecclesiastics," as Derek Pearsall points out. So much so that "the principle memory of reading 'The General Prologue' is of the detailed and minute revelation of ecclesiastical malpractice... This is a mark of the suitability of such malpractice to satirical observation, and not necessarily an indication that Chaucer had an opinion of the church lower than most of his contemporaries (this would still make it pretty low), but it does serve also as a measure of the extent to which fourteenth-century life was saturated in the influence of the church, its practices, regulations, writings, and daily and seasonal rhythms." ∎

found them expressed on a stained glass window there" representing the wedding at Cana and an inscription pointing to the allegorical meaning of the wine.

In other words, Chaucer's readers, not to mention the other pilgrims, probably knew enough of the standard teaching on marriage to realise how off-base the Wife is. Is she ignorant of Biblical exegesis? Her adroit use of the text "God bad us for to wexe and multiplye" (28) suggests not. Is she devious? Her reception by the other pilgrims suggests no hostility.

What is more likely is that she is enjoying a huge, elaborate joke at the expense of scholarly interpreters:

But yet I praye to al this compaignye.
If that I speke after my fantasye,
As taketh not agrief of that I saye,
For myn entente nys but for to pleye.
                    [189-189]

Here is the place to add that the Wife also has another 'estate' – not a contemporary social role this time but a traditional literary one. As a literary figure she derives from *La Vieille*, the Old Woman in the widely read 'The Romance of the Rose', the part written by Jean de Meun in about 1275. *La Vieille* was an accepted literary expression of what age could contribute to the wisdom of love. Long before the Wife, she too was offering advice to the youth on the superiority of experience over book-learning, recounting her own youth and the woes of marriage.

So the Wife of Bath has literary tradition behind her. That's part of what makes her so convincing "on the page", but only part. Another part is her verbal energy, and her fluid phrasing. Part of this latter effect is produced by the prosody: she is given more run-on lines than most characters in *The Canterbury Tales*, most of whom have to plod along with end stops. So from the very beginning of her Prologue, "Experience" vanquishes "auctoritee" even as it cuts across the regular metre. And the same happens in her very funny discourse on the use of the sexual parts:

> *Glose [gloss, interpret] whoso wole, and*
> *seye bothe up and doun*
> *That they were maked for purgacioun*
> *Of uryne, and oure bothe thynges smale*
> *Were eek to knowe a femele from a male,*
> *And for noon oother cause – say ye no?*
> *The experience woot well it is noght so,* [119-124]

Above all, what makes the Wife so convincing is her abundant generosity of spirit. Unlike January in 'The Merchant's Tale', so meanly calculating in his quest for "wedlock" as a way of making sex "esy and so clene" (1264), she "ne loved nevere by no discrecioun" (622), and married her fifth husband "for love and no richesse" (526). And once Jankyn burns the book that has caused her so much "wo", as Carolyn Dinshaw puts it, her Prologue ends with the strong suggestion "that what she wants is reciprocity; despite her talk of maistrie;* she most wants mutual recognition and satisfaction of desires".

How is her tale connected to the Prologue?

Derek Pearsall thinks that the Wife's tale ends on that same note of reciprocity. "The suggestion must be," he writes, "that, though the old hag (who is also the Wife of Bath) speaks the language of sovereignty, what she really seeks is the recognition by the man of the individuality, the inward reality, of her existence as a person." This judgement is right. How does the tale produce it?

With its knightly test and its transformation of the old hag into the beautiful young woman, 'The Wife of Bath's Tale' is a sort of fairy story. Yet Chaucer has changed his most likely source, 'The Tale of Florent' in John Gower's 'Confessio Amantis' (1390). In the Chaucer version, the Knight has committed the sin and crime of rape, robbing a defenceless maiden of her virginity,

*Mastery, or control in marriage.

whereas Florent has killed another (well defended) knight in chivalric combat. Also in the Gower story the ugly old hag turns young and beautiful before offering Florent the choice (a different one from that in the Wife's tale) of having her lovely by day and lothly at night, or the other way round.

Most important, though, is that Chaucer's takes up over a quarter of the tale to lecture the Knight on *gentillese* – a subject not even mentioned in the Gower. Why? It has to do with yet another departure from the source. In Gower what deters the Knight's desire for the lady are her looks and age, as set out in truly loathsome detail.* In Chaucer the predominant issue is her class; the Knight objects to the hag's low background.

She answers that to assume that "gentilesse" arises from "old richesse" is "arrogance... nat worth an hen" (1109-1112), and goes on to illustrate the point, quoting Dante, Valerius, Seneca and Boethius, over the next 103 highly convincing lines. When finally they turn to the topic of her appearance, she says that to say "that I am foul and old" means he will never "been a cokewold" (1213-1214), then goes on to offer him the choice – a more profound *questione d'amore* than the choice offered the knight in Gower – of having her old, ugly and true, or young, beautiful and false (1219-1226).

*'The Tale of Florent' is also reprinted in NCE, 386-96.

So a story that begins with a man exercising the most violent power over a beautiful young woman ends with him ceding the *maistrie* to an ugly old hag. What changes his mind (if 'mind' is the right word) is the old woman's long, reasonable – even moving – discourse on inner worth as compared to externals such as rank, age and looks. In other words, her fairy-tale transformation is nothing to his more realistic transformation from snobbish rapist to patient apprentice in the art of true love.

But this is nothing compared to the transformation that takes place between teller and tale. Pearsall says the old hag is also the Wife of Bath. But the Wife's Prologue is an energetic, witty defence of the literal over the figurative. For her it's the flesh that makes life interesting, while the old woman arranges her whole story around the lesson that true value lies in the spirit. Does this sea change have anything to do with the magic worked in 'The Wife of Bath's Tale'?

The Franklin's Tale

Averagus marries Dorigen, a Breton princess, promising never to give her orders, apart from those relating to his feudal status. When he crosses the channel to England in search of fame through knightly combat, she pines for him, fixating on a field of rocks off the coast as symbolic barrier to his return. When a young squire called Aurelius pays

court to her, Dorigen playfully tells him,
little thinking that he can manage the feat, that
if he can make the rocks go away, she will accede
to his desires.

But when Aurelius hires a young scholar to
work his astrological tables so that the rocks really
do vanish, or at least appear to, Dorigen thinks
herself forced to choose between her marriage
vows and her word to the squire. On returning
home Averagus surprises her by insisting she
keep to her bargain with Aurelius. When Aurelius
realises how much she loves her husband and how
much both are giving up, he relinquishes his part
of the deal. Impressed by this renunciation, the
scholar waives his fee, and everything ends happily.
The question is posed: which of them was most
generous; who gave up the most?

How seriously should we take the Franklin?

What sort of thing is 'The Franklin's Tale'? It
pretends to be a Breton lay or lai, but it shares few
characteristics of that genre. It isn't particularly
sing-able, or in eight-syllable lines, or about the
realm of faerie or – except fragmentarily – a
romance. It does end with that question, which
makes it one of those *demandes d'amour*, questions
about love, (or *questioni d'amore* if you lived in
Italy) – that courtly people liked to hear and

debate. Boccaccio wrote two of them, one in *Il Filocolo* (1336-1339) and another in *Il Decamerone* (1351-1353).

In *Il Decamerone* (tenth day, fifth tale), it's a summer garden in winter for which the lady pines – a garden as warm, sunny and flowery in January as in May. Her would-be lover works the illusion through a necromancer, thus winning the right to the lady's bed. Her husband gives her leave to keep her bargain, but the lover, moved by the husband's liberality, absolves her from her promise, and so does the necromancer the lover from his debt. The 'court' judges the lover to have been most liberal, because while the marital affection had cooled, the lover loved "più ferventamente che mai amando e quasi da più speranza acceso".*

On the fourth day of *Il Filocolo*, a longer version of the same story line ends in the verdict that the husband is the most generous, because his honour, once given up, could not have been regained.** In the context of *The Canterbury Tales,* 'The Franklin's Tale' was thought by George Lyman Kittredge to be the happy resolution to a debate on marriage among the pilgrims specifically as to whether the husband should exert *maistrie* over

*'more fervently than ever, being inflamed by greater expectation'.

**Both these analogues to 'The Franklin's Tale' can be found on the Harvard Chaucer Page for 'The Franklin's Tale', www.courses.fas.harvard.edu/~chaucer/canttales/franklin/

the wife or vice versa. In his highly influential essay on "Chaucer's Discussion of Marriage" (1911-1912), Kittredge argued that the marriage contract in which the husband promises to be his wife's servant in love but her lord in marriage is tested and proved by the tale that follows. "For the marriage of Averagus and Dorigen was a brilliant success," he says. "Thus the whole debate has been brought to a satisfactory conclusion, and the Marriage Act of the Human Comedy ends with the conclusion of the Franklin's Tale."

In his *A Preface to Chaucer* D. W. Robertson takes a completely contrary line. "It is clearly impossible to be a 'servant' in love and 'lord' in marriage at the same time," he says, "except under the conditions like those arranged in this instance, where the husband keeps only the 'name' of lordship." As for the *questione* of which character is the most generous, "no one in the tale gives up anything he has any real right to hold, so that no one is actually generous".

Robertson bases his attack on the supposed generosity in the 'The Franklin's Tale' on exegetical distinctions such as that between the literal meaning and the intention of Dorigen's bargain with Aurelius. Another exegetical reading yielding quite different results can be found in Gerald Morgan's "Boccaccio's *Filocolo* and the Moral Argument of the *Franklin's Tale*". Unlike Robertson and, for that matter, Derek Pearsall,

Morgan takes the *questione* seriously; he thinks the tale really is about generosity, which, in the case of Averagus, "is a donnée [given] of the tale", the seed from which the story grew. To read for character rather than action, he thinks, is a modern critical aberration.

Harry Berger, Jr embraces that critical aberration with a vengeance. His "Pleasure and Responsibility in the Franklin's Tale" concentrates on the Franklin himself, almost as a character in a novel: his likes and dislikes, his brief dismissal of – or "soft focus on [–] the various dilemmas and contradictions in his tale". So it follows that "the Franklin's interruptions during the central portion of the tale do not strike us as primarily intended to produce certain effects on his audience; they seem rather to rise from the effects of the tale on him". As for the question of generosity, this seems intended to stir up a debate "not among Chaucer's readers, but among the Franklin's auditors".

Perhaps the most productive approach to 'The Franklin's Tale' would be to start with the Franklin, but not as a character so much as a kind of storyteller – precisely, that is, from the standpoint of his effort to produce certain effects on his audience, as well as on us, the readers of the tale. Above all, though he disclaims all arts of rhetoric, this is a narrator determined to tell his tale tricked out with ambitious rhetorical devices, though he doesn't always manage the effect intended. For example, he produces an inadvertently comic effect when he tries to illustrate the incompatibility between romantic or courtly love and the feudal order.

> *Whan maistrie comth, the God of Love anon*
> *Beteth [beats] his wynges, and farewel, he is gon!*
> *[765-766]*

You can see what he is trying for – the image of winged Eros or Cupid fleeing the scene in delicate aversion – but here the god looks more like a large, unwieldy scavenger, perhaps a vulture taking to the air.

Here the manner mirrors an uncertain matter, because the Franklin is clearly having trouble explaining the compromise between love and lordship:

> *Heere may men seen an humble, wys accord;*
> *Thus hath she take hir servant and hir lord –*
> *Servant in love and lord in mariage.*
> *Thanne was he bothe in lordshipe and servage.*
> *Servage? Nay, but in lordshipe above,*
> *Sith [since] he hath bothe his lady and his love;*
> *His lady, certes and his wyf also,*
> *The which that lawe of love acordeth to [791-798]*

The ways this exposition advances and retreats, backs and fills, suggest that the Franklin might have been anticipating Professor Robertson's judgement that this contract is invalidated by its contradictions. And of course Robertson is right. In Chaucer and the Middle Ages generally, courtly love, in which the man played the servant, was typically an adulterous relationship between a suitor of inferior (yet still courtly) rank and the wife of his feudal lord.

Marriage was and is still a sacrament based on the relationship between Christ and the Church, in which the wife obeyed her husband and the husband loved his wife as his own body. Within that bond there could be mutual love and trust of the sort explored in the Wife of Bath's fairy tale

POETICS AND METRICS

Chaucer inherited two verse traditions. One, from the Old English, used non-rhyming lines in which certain words were linked by alliteration and the stresses counted, not the syllables. The other, featuring eight-syllable lines arranged in rhyming couplets, came from French and Latin models.

The first of these he used only once, when he wanted to add epic dimensions to the climactic tournament between Palamon and Arcite in 'The Knight's Tale' (line 2603 and following). The latter is the verse form of some of his early poems, like 'The Book of the Duchesse' and 'The House of Fame'.

Chaucer also developed another French form, later to

and (less conventionally) in her own life, but there could be no compromise between servant and love and lord in marriage without splitting love and marriage into separate spheres of emotional experience and hence behaviour.

In the 14th and 15th centuries franklins were landowners, free but not noble. Yet for this Franklin *franchise* (nobility of character) and *gentilesse* are near synonyms, as he makes clear in line 1524, and his question at the end, which of the characters is "mooste fre?" (1622), is at least partly tied up in his own self image. 'The General Prologue' describes him as a great householder, a generous host, a lover of good food and wine – "Epicurus owene sone" for whom "pleyn delit/ Was verray felicitee parfit" (336-338). In other

---

be called the rime royal. This was a seven-line stanza with five beats, rhyming a-b-a-b-b-c-c. He used it in 'Troilus and Criseyde', 'The Parliament of Fowls' and four of *The Canterbury Tales*: The Man of Law's, The Clerk's, The Prioress' and The Second Nun's.

His distinctive style, though, and his great poetic innovation, used with increasing variety and fluidity in *The Canterbury Tales*, was the rhyming couplet of five stress lines that would become the standard for heroic and satiric verse in modern English, from Christopher Marlowe's mini-epic 'Hero and Leander' (1598), down through the great satiric and philosophical verse essays of John Dryden and Alexander Pope.

In these later hands the heroic couplet would become regularised as composed of lines of iambic pentameter – that is, each with five two-syllable feet, each

words, he followed the Greek philosopher who taught that pleasure was the highest good. His complexion is "sangwyn" (333), and so is his disposition. An optimist, he is also highly conscious of his social status. This would account for his wish to approve of Dorigen's and Averagus's unusual marriage contract, and also his uncertainty in trying to justify it.

Here is the place to point out that those "grisly rokkes blake" exist in the real life, as a partly submerged reef between Jersey and St Malo. They are called *les Minquiers* in the local dialect of French, and the Minkies in English. Because the tidal range in that region is one of the greatest on

---

containing one unstressed and one stressed syllable in that order. With Chaucer, though, you should count the beats, not the syllables. For example, in 'The Merchant's Tale', when the elderly January first has sex with young May on their wedding night, he tries to reassure her that:

> In trewe wedlok coupled be we tweye [two]
> And blessed be the yok that we been inne.
> For in oure actes we mowe [may] do no synne.
> [1836-1838]

It would be hard to scan this as regular iambic pentameter. The voiced terminal 'e's turn the word in which they occur into a trochaic foot – a stressed followed by an unstressed syllable – and almost always make the line spill over the standard ten syllables. The first two lines quoted above contain 11, and the third 12. But concentrate on the stresses, and there are (almost) always five ∎

earth – 12 metres, or some six times the world average – the sea moves in or out between these rocks and islets in terrific swirls and whirlpools. Any vessel attempting to navigate through them – apart from a kayak in calm weather and good visibility, a popular local sport – would be sure to fetch up on one of them. So mariners give the Minkies a wide berth.

But because the tides are so extreme there, the Minkies seem to grow and shrink astonishingly. At low tide the reef is about 100 square miles in area; at spring highs there is only one tiny island, less than a tenth of a square mile showing above the surface.

Did Chaucer know this maritime lore? It certainly seems so, given the way he articulates the "magic" worked by the astrologer, who in effect coordinates his various tables to find an extreme high tide that will submerge the rocks – not permanently but "for a wyke or tweye" so that "It semed that alle the rokkes were aweye" (1296). "Semed" is the key, of course. For the narrator tells us in two places (1264 and 1293) that the effect is an illusion. And a danger to shipping, too, making the "rokkes blake", like the Minkies, even more of a threat, since ships sailing over them unaware would have their bottoms torn out.

Which is what makes Averagus's *sentence*, sonorously proclaimed to his wife – "Trouthe is the hyeste thyng that man may kepe" (1479) – so fatuous. The ironies undermining it are almost too numerous to list. First, it's a truth that he wants to hide, since he immediately cautions her to keep it quiet, "'up peyne of deeth'" (1481). Second, he is counselling Dorigen to negate their marriage "trouthe". Third, Dorigen's bargain with Aurelius – "'Have heer my trouthe, in al that evere I kan'" (998) – was based on the premise that he would remove the rocks, a result that would hasten her husband's safe return. Fourth, he didn't remove the rocks, but only pretended to.

But of course that bargain was bogus to begin with. When Aurelius first propositions Dorigen, she repels him with "'Ne shal I nevere been untrewe wyf'" (984). Then she offers the removal of- the-rocks deal, but "in pley" (988), not seriously. He takes this as the rebuke it is meant to be – "'Is ther noon oother grace in yow?' quod he" (998) – to which she answers, just in case he's in any doubt:

> *"No, by that Lord,' quod she, 'that maked me!*
> *For wel I woot [know] that it shal never bityde*
> > *[happen].*
> *Lat swich folies out of youre herte slyde.*
> *What deyntee sholde a man han in his lyf*
> *For to go love another mannes wyf."*
> > *[999-1004]*

How real is Dorigen's dilemma?

So it's all the more surprising, given her firm grip on reality here, that Dorigen comes to accept her dilemma as a real one. In her un-Boethian complaint beginning on 1355 she says she has been wrapped "unwar" in Fortune's chain, and that she has been left no choice save "'deeth or elles dishonour'", both of which claims are untrue. Forced to a false conclusion by this wholly abstract logic, she now has only one further choice to make: how to do herself in. Her readings in classical antiquity offer endless examples of women who preferred death to dishonour. There's Lucretia, of course, and the seven maids of Miletus and not just one but two Theban maidens, and Portia who could not live without Brutus, not to mention Hasdrubal's wife who, when the Romans captured Carthage:

> *"Took hir children alle, and skipte adoun*
> *Into the fyr, and chees rather to dye*
> *Than any Romayn dide here vileynye."*
> *[1402-1404]*

Here the Franklin's rhetoric is slipping again, not only with that slightly too jolly run-on about the lady and her children skipping down into the fire, but also with the lack of shape to Dorigen's complaint overall. She could go on forever –indeed says as much, when she seems to draw it to a close with "What sholde I mo ensamples heerof sayn" (1419) – only to re-launch herself into another 70 lines in the same vein. Indeed, it is only the return home of her husband that stops her, after, we are told, she had been complaining "*a day or tweye*" (1457, my italics).

It's clear she doesn't really want to kill herself, or even see the reason why she should. As Harry Berger puts it: "This is a Scheherazade situation in parody:* Dorigen feels capable of going through 'mo than a thousand stories'... until Averagus comes home". In other words, Dorigen's instincts – her trust in and loyal love for her husband, her life-enhancing spirit – are a good deal sounder than the various catastrophes drawn from history. And this is especially true of the absurd marriage contract with which it all begins, that modish notion of living a courtly romance in real life. Theoretically shot through with contradictions, it is nevertheless validated by Dorigen's and Averagus's love for one another: love in the sense of *agape* or charity as well as of eros, sexual attraction as represented in the literature of courtly love.

*In the sense that she must tell a beguiling story in order to put off being killed by her husband in the morning, from the Arabic collection of tales, *A Thousand and One Nights*, translated into English as *The Arabian Nights*.

What is the lesson of 'The Franklin's Tale'?

That same sense of sound humanity underlying the absurdity of progressive theory redeems the decisions made by all those who relinquish their claims at the end. They may have no right, as Robertson says, to the things they offer to give up, but in their Epicurean ignorance of the distinction between letter and spirit, they think they do, and therefore their sacrifice is genuine. That's what makes the ending of the tale feel so much more humane than that of – say – 'The Merchant's Tale', with the mean-spirited January getting the biter-bit treatment. Here, by contrast, the giver gives – or at least thinks he does.

Of the various lessons advertised in 'The Franklin's Tale' – the debate over generosity, the sentence about "trouthe" – the one that survives the test of experience is the encomium to patience from lines 772 to 786. Patience is "an heigh virtu" because it accomplishes things that moral harshness and theoretical vigour could "nevere atteyne". We must all learn to suffer reverses, or we will learn the lesson whether we want to or not:

> *For in this world, certain, ther no wight*
> > *[person] is*
> *That he ne dooth or seith somtyme amys.*
> *Ire, sicknesse, or constellacioun*

[fate, as determined by the stars],
Wyn [Wine], wo [woe], or chaungynge of
complexioun [emotional balance]
Causeth ful ofte to doon amys or speken.
On every wrong a man may nat be wreken
[avenged],
After [according to] the tyme moste be
temperaunce [moderation]
To every wight that can on governaunce.
[understands self control]

[779-786]

This follows the Franklin's botched attempt to
rationalise the terms of Dorigen's and Averagus's
wedding. No character speaks it, so it is not part
of a partisan appeal. It has no obvious connection
with what comes before or after it. Instead it
comes over as somewhat disembodied, not to say
objective, as though it could be applied to any and
all aspects of 'The Franklin's Tale' – the threat of
the "grisly rokkes blak", the crosses of Fortune,
the contradictions of the various compacts struck
throughout the story, Dorigen's 'dilemma', all of
them more apparent than real, none of them
insuperable with love, charity and patience. Here,
where moral and story are truly interfused, lies the
profundity of 'The Franklin's Tale'.

The Pardoner's Tale

In his Prologue the Pardoner reveals how he stage-manages his profitable sermons on the theme of *radix malorum est cupiditas* (greed is the root of all evil). The trick is to mix fancy words and a little Latin with jokes and old stories, then to show his relics and sell pardons.

His tale begins with a vivid attack on gluttony, gambling and swearing before embarking on an exemplary story about three young thugs who set out from a tavern to find Death and kill him. An old man, who wants to die but can't, directs them up a crooked path to an old oak tree, under which they find a treasure of gold and coin. While one of the three goes into town to get food, he decides to poison the drink he's bought, so that after the others have drunk, he can have the treasure all for himself.

Meanwhile the other two plan to kill him when he returns. This they do, then sit down to drink, and die. So all three find death. After he has told his tale, the Pardoner sets out his relics for the other pilgrims to venerate, provoking an obscene rejection from the Host.

How much does the Pardoner's sexuality matter?

Like the Wife of Bath, the Pardoner is allowed an extensive *apologia pro vita sua* that has prompted critical comment on all aspects of his person. On a line running from allegorical figure to novelistic character, however, the Wife comes much closer to the latter polarity. As Derek Pearsall has written, "she speaks constantly of her thoughts and feelings, her hopes and regrets: she does not always speak consistently or honestly, but it is in that region of inner being that she moves".

The Pardoner, by contrast, "has no thoughts or feelings... no hopes or regrets. He never talks about his motives, except to reiterate monotonously that his purpose is ever one. He never once says 'I think' or 'I feel', but only describes what he has done or what he will do." Yet within that narrow range of self-proclaimed intention the Pardoner creates the irony in which he speaks the truth in order to deceive. In this he is like False Seeming in the 'Romance of the Rose', whose candour proclaims what he stands for, as with any allegorical figure, but also invites others to share the joke, thus tempting them to accept his duplicity:

> But however much I pretend to be poor, I pay no attention to any poor person. I would a hundred thousand times prefer the acquaintance of the King of France to that of a poor man, by our lady, even though he had as good a soul.
>
> ('Romance of the Rose' 1135-1139)

And so, as D. W. Robertson writes in *A Preface to Chaucer,* "[t]he pardoner makes it abundantly clear that although he knows the implications of *radix malorum est cupiditas,* cupidity is nevertheless his prime motivation in life". Robertson's main focus is on the tale, which he sees as a Christian morality play, with the old man recalling the Old Man in Ephesians 4.22, himself a personification of the old manner of life that St Paul enjoins us to put behind us.

Where the Pardoner does take on a dimension additional to the presentation of False Seeming is in his supposed sexuality. This has aroused enormous critical attention. In 'The General Prologue', where he is the last of the pilgrims to be described, certain personal details accompany those references to the tricks of his trade (his wallet stuffed with pardons, his jar full of "pigges bones" offered as relics of the saints, and so on). His hair is unbound and yellow as wax (675-676); his eyes glare like a hare's (648); his voice is high (688) and he has no beard (689). "I trowe [guess] he were a geldyng or a mare" (691), adds the Narrator, Chaucer's persona. This has been taken to mean either a eunuch or a homosexual.

The remark is a bit confusing. Though the beardlessness and high-pitched voice might square with castration before puberty, it certainly doesn't suggest homosexuality. Clearly what we have here is another of those Rumsfeldian unknowns, like his not knowing the Merchant's name, except that this time he is less explicit. The Narrator either doesn't know if the Pardoner is a eunuch or a homosexual, or thinks he does but doesn't – or doesn't care.

Not that this uncertainty or inattention has deterred the critics from offering definite diagnoses of the Pardoner's condition. Walter Clyde Curry was one of the earliest diagnosticians to think the Pardoner's sexuality central to the meaning of both his Prologue and Tale. Drawing on his knowledge of the medieval sciences, he states that the Pardoner is a *eunuchus ex nativitate*, in modern terms either a male child born without testicles or a man whose testicles failed to develop at puberty.

Also opting for the eunuch diagnosis is Carolyn Dinshaw. The chapter 'Eunuch Hermenutics' in

THE TABARD INN AND THE SINK OF SOUTHWARK

Pilgrims on their way from London to Canterbury set off from Southwark, just across the Thames at the southern end of London Bridge. This is because they needed to get an early start, before the bridge gatehouses were unlocked. For the same reason anyone arriving late from the South or East would need to find a place to stay over until they were opened in the morning. Hence the high number of inns and taverns like the Tabard, along the road leading south from the bridge, now the Borough

her *Chaucer's Sexual Poetics* starts by suggesting that the Pardoner's loss was the literal re-enactment of that Freudian primal scene in which the child first notices its mother's lack of a penis, so comes to fear a similar 'castration' at the hands of its father. Consequently the Pardoner, who will later be threatened with actual castration by the Host, accumulates fetishes "– relics, sealed documents, even language regarded as a kind of object – that he substitutes for his own lacking parts. But these objects are themselves fragments, and cannot properly fill the lack that hollows the pardoner's being." Monica McAlpine concentrates on the 'Mare' half of the Narrator's designation. Her essay on "The Pardoner's Homosexuality and How it Matters" seeks to open up the possible implications of homosexuality for the man himself.

High Street.

But Southwark was also home to late-night activities other than sleeping, like heavy drinking, gambling, bear baiting, popular entertainment in the taverns and prostitution in the "stews" nearby. And it was all as legal as an offshore tax haven, since Southwark was made up of a number of "liberties" – that is, precincts outside the jurisdiction of the mother city across the river.

There was the Paris Garden Liberty, the Mint Liberty, the Clink Liberty, even a Liberty of the Archbishop of Canterbury. In the Mint people in debt could evade their creditors. In the Clink they might find themselves in an especially damp prison that spawned the phrase "in the clink", or frequenting one of a number of brothels owned and

The key to the Pardoner's behaviour, she thinks, is "the shame that attends the naming of the sin even in the confessional". So "[i]t is no accident that the man who cannot confess becomes a pardoner".

C. David Benson is having none of this. His essay, "Chaucer's Pardoner: His Sexuality and Modern Critics", dismisses all this preoccupation with the Pardoner's sexuality. Neither "geldyng" nor "mare" mean what modern critics think they do, he writes, but "may simply indicate that the Pardoner is effeminate in some way". Although there is clearly something odd about the Pardoner, "his sexuality remains too imprecise to serve as a reliable guide to his entire performance and tale".

Then, in "The Sexual Normality of Chaucer's Pardoner", Richard Firth Green stands the whole diagnostic enterprise on its head by claiming that

managed by the Bishop of Winchester.

That's right, the Bishop of Winchester controlled the area's prostitutes. Indeed, in one way or another religion was heavily involved in Southwark. Grandees of the church, like the Abbot of St Augustine's in Canterbury, the Prior of St Pancras and the Bishop of Winchester himself had their town houses there.

Inns started out as religious establishments that welcomed guests in return for payment. The Tabard, where Chaucer's pilgrims meet and start their journey, began as an offshoot of a hostel set up by the Abbot of Hyde and his brethren to stay in when they had business in London. Inns along the High Street, like the Tabard, the Catherine Wheel, the Crossed Keys and the White

the glaring eyes, flaxen hair and high voice all indicate too *much* indulgence in heterosexual sex, not too little. Like Absolon in 'The Miller's Tale', the Pardoner has been debilitated by sexual excess. Green takes seriously the Pardoner's boastful claim to have "a joly wenche in every toun" (453), rather than as cover for homosexual encounters, or compensation for no sex at all. His "compeer" the Summoner, Green points out, is a "good felawe" – a common phrase for a sexual adventurer – and the two pals "have much in common with the three rioters of the Pardoner's own tale".

Probably the most balanced view of the Pardoner's sexuality and what it means in its historical context is set out in Lee Patterson's 2002 essay, "The Pardoner's Dilemma". "In late

---

Hart shared a similar architecture. The visitor entered from the street via a narrow passageway under an arch into a large yard surrounded on three sides by stables and offices on the ground floor, with galleried guest rooms above them. Today only the George Inn, of 75-77 Borough High Street, survives as a reminder of the medieval galleried inns.

Guests in the Southwark inns were entertained by strolling musicians, acrobats and play actors, three further activities outlawed from central London. In the 16th century, long after Chaucer's death, the galleried inns would form the model for the Southwark Bankside playhouses like the Rose and the Globe owned and used by Shakespeare and his contemporaries ∎

Medieval England castration was virtually unknown," he writes, and "sodomy, as either social practice or ideological construct, was not a major presence in Chaucer's cultural world".

But mention of either or both could register symbolically. "Sodomy was reviled because it was unproductive; the Pardoner is sterile rather than queer, but spiritually so." Reformist theologians used sodomy as a figure for simony, which meant not just the buying and selling of church offices, but "the selling of any spiritual good for a material reward". And the selling of indulgences was "the grossest form of simony", because it displaces true contrition for pieces of parchment, the spirit for the letter.

So *can* a bad man tell a moral tale?

The Wife of Bath, who is neither a man nor wholly bad, tells a tale that exemplifies the opposite of what she stands for. Her Prologue is a witty defence of literal over spiritual meanings, while the loathly lady of the tale teaches the Knight how inner worth can triumph over surface appearance. The Pardoner's contrast is much more explicit: he boasts that he can "preche agayn [against] that same vice/Which that I use, and that is avarice" (427-428).

The question can be considered on both theological and aesthetic levels. Theologically

The Pardoner (centre), engraving, William Blake, 1810

speaking, the issue was whether a wicked priest
could preach or administer the sacraments.
According to Alistair Minnis, whose *Fallible
Authors* deals with both the Pardoner and the
Wife of Bath, the fifth-century Pope Leo I worked
out a theory by which the subjective personality
of the man was distinct from the objective office
he discharged. Much later the philosopher and
scholastic theologian St Thomas Aquinas worked
this idea into the "principle of instrumentality",

whereby the minister was thought to be merely the instrument moved by another power. A doctor may himself be ill, but that doesn't prevent him from making others well.

But what about preaching? "Here the instrument argument is shakier," Minnis writes, "because preaching demands the confidence of the audience." A preacher *widely known* to be immoral might well scandalise the congregation. "Acutely aware of this problem, the Schoolmen put themselves in a difficult (if not ethically dubious) position by promoting a policy of 'Don't ask, don't tell'."

By Chaucer's time, however, theological reformers were "beginning to blow away all these cobwebs of schoolmen thinking". John

---

THE ROUTE: HOW THE PILGRIMS GOT TO CANTERBURY

Canterbury is around 60 miles east of London; so the pilgrims could do the journey in four days, with three overnight stops.

Heading east from Southwark along the south bank of the Thames, they would pass through Deptford, then Greenwich. After that they would follow the old Roman Watling Street, though by the 14th century its pavement had so badly deteriorated that riders and walkers were forced off onto parallel tracks here and there. The present-day A-2 follows the same route.

Wycliffe, who translated the Latin Vulgate Bible into English in 1382, argued in his treatise, *Of Prelates*, that "a prest may be so cursed & in heresie that he makith not the sacrament". Patterson, too, suggests that there was "a widespread discourse of spiritual or religious sterility that fits the Pardoner with surprising aptness. This discourse, sometimes labelled Wycliffite or Lollard, might better be called, more simply and broadly, 'reformist'." Chaucer would have shared "some aspects of this reformist impulse".

The Pardoner's sermons, especially, would have aroused the hostility of the reformers. "False preaching" – so as to attract money from the audience, or that strayed from exposition of

---

Their first night they might spend in Dartford, an important market town some 15 miles from London. It was well adapted for pilgrim travel, and a number of religious houses stood ready to welcome those who wished to avoid the rougher trade. Fifteen miles further on their second night's rest might be in the city of Rochester.

Their third day's trek would be the longest: 20-odd miles through Sittingbourne to Ospringe, today a tiny village of just over 700 residents, immediately south of present-day Faversham. There the pilgrims might have stayed in a religious hostelry called the Maison Dieu [House of God], which is still standing and can be visited.

The fourth day would be their last, a fairly easy leg of the route of around 12 miles, through Boughton-under-Blean and Harbledown,

the biblical text into jokes, gossip and fables – was considered the worst form of simony. Even exempla were suspect, Patterson adds, noting that the Parson's sermon-like tale is almost entirely devoid of exempla, while the Pardoner's is one long one.

So by Chaucer's time the theological position was swinging against the possibility that a bad man could tell a good tale. But what about the aesthetic position? In other words, what about the Pardoner and his tale as realised in Chaucer's fiction? Derek Traversi is in no doubt as to the answer: "the moral of the tale, superbly conveyed as it is in the telling, is invalidated by the self-confessed perversity of the teller".

But let's unpick that judgement, starting with

---

to Canterbury.

These waymarks get mentioned from time to time in the framing narrative of *The Canterbury Tales*. Squabbling with the Friar at the end of 'The Wife of Bath's Prologue', the Summoner threatens to "telle tales two or thre/Of freres er I come to Sidyngborne" (846-847). After he makes good his threat (he even tells one of his anti-friar jokes in his Prologue), he finally signs off

with: "My tale is doon; we been almoost attowne" (2294).

On the fourth day, before they had ridden barely five miles from Ospringe, the pilgrims are overtaken by the Canon: "At Boughtoun under Blee us gan atake/A man that clothed was in clothes blake" (556-557). Later the Canon's Yeoman tells the pilgrims that he had seen them ride "Out of youre hostelrie" that morning (589).

the status of the Pardoner himself, if not as full-blown character, then at least as an individualised narrative presence – 'narrative', that is, in both the sense of how he is realised within the narrative of *The Canterbury Tales* and also in how he himself tells a story.

For Pearsall the Pardoner is "dead", a figure of "vacuity", of "unspeakable evil"; for Minnis he is "an exceptionally vicious man": all fair enough judgements, perhaps. But then Minnis goes on to call him "the most offensive character on [Chaucer's] pilgrimage". What, more offensive than the Summoner in 'The Friar's Tale', who serves false summonses on the poor? Or January in 'The Merchant's Tale', who marries a young woman for sex that's "esy and clene"? Or Absolon,

---

Still further on, now only two miles from Canterbury, the Host jokes on the name of Harbledown:

Woot ye nat where ther stant a litel toun Which that ycleped [called] is Bobbe-up-and-doun' Under the Blee, in Canterbury Weye?
'The Manciple's Prologue', [1-3]

All these references seem more or less in order, if hardly instrumental to the framing narrative. Somewhat stranger is the first mention of a place along the route. "Lo Depeford, and it is half-wey pryme!" says the Host, reproving the pilgrims for dragging their feet. Which is odd, since it's only 7:30 in the morning, and it takes a good hour and a half to walk, or ride at walking pace, from London Bridge to Deptford

for whom itching at the lips is a sign of "kissing atte leest"?

To be sure, the Pardoner does describe himself as "a ful vicious man" (459), but that degree of self-knowledge, if nothing more, sets him apart from those other three. The same is true of the self-confessed False Seeming. Does this transparency with respect to those they encounter make them less wicked, or more so? Less "offensive" at least, I think.

Besides, the Pardoner's self knowledge goes further than False Seeming's. He "serves to demonstrate the truth of reformist claims about empty formalism", as Patterson puts it, "not merely by displaying them but by internalising them". He not only demonstrates the death of the

---

(did they set out at five?), and already they have heard the Knight and Miller tell their stories.

Another oddity with the framing narrative is that the pilgrims don't appear ever to reach their goal, Canterbury itself. When the Manciple finishes his Tale, the Narrator gives an elaborate set of formulae to tell us what time it is (the sun has dropped to 29 degrees above the horizon, casting a man's shadow of eleven feet, etc., etc.), which is to say it was four o'clock in the afternoon – all this just as "we were entryng a thorpes ende" [the edge of a village]. But which "thorp" would that be?

So the time is ponderously established, but not the place. Instead of the shrine of the "hooly blisful martir", we (and the pilgrims) get the rigours of 'The Parson's Tale' ∎

soul; he experiences it. "He is therefore not merely in danger of damnation but knows of his danger, indeed focuses upon it with excessive anxiety."

Does the Pardoner's perversity really undermine the tale?

No, for two reasons. The first is that the tale really is "superbly conveyed... in the telling", as Traversi admits, and although Chaucer would have nearly 500 years to wait before D. H. Lawrence famously said "Never trust the teller; trust the tale", he would – as a gifted, experienced and ambitious artist acquainted with the theology of subjective personality and objective office – never have shrunk from the challenge of exploring the aesthetic side of the issue, proving the truth that fiction can tell. The second is that the tale fits the teller because it is really a coded expression of the Pardoner's psychic state.

The best way to explore the tale is to take it in three parts: the diatribe against gluttony, gambling and swearing; the exemplum of the three louts in search of Death; and the mysterious figure of the old man who wants to die but can't.

To mount the diatribe the Pardoner invokes all his rhetorical skill – his vigorous rhythms, vivid imagery and daring mixture of concrete and abstract:

Allas, a foul thyng is it, by my feith,
To seye this word, and fouler is the dede,
When man so drynketh of the white and red
           [wines]
That of his throte he maketh his privee
         [privy, toilet]
Thurgh thilke [this] cursed superfluitee...
O wombe! O bely! O stynkyng cod [bag]
Fulfilled of dong and of corrupcioun!
At either ende of thee foul is the soun [sound].
           [524-536]

And, by the way, gluttony is not a vice indulged in by the Pardoner, so far as we know, so here he is not "preche[ing] agayn that same vice/Which that I use, and that is avarice".

The exemplum is one of dozens of tales with the same story line,* from ancient tales to the classic Walter Huston movie of 1948, *The Treasure of the Sierra Madre*, starring Humphrey Bogart, Tim Holt and Huston himself. So the powerful irony of the futile search for, and unexpected encounter, with Death comes with the traditional tale. Chaucer's Pardoner intensifies the moral by having the thugs swear "many a grisly ooth" (708), and ends with the curt couplet –

*See, for example, "The Hermit, Death and the Robbers", translated by V. A. Kolve, in NCE, 436 – 38; also the analogues under 'The Pardoner's Tale' in the Harvard Chaucer Page.

Thus ended been thise homycides two,
And eek [even] the false empoysonere also.
[893-894]

– before dissipating the tension in a welter of windy apostrophes ("O cursed synne... O wikkednesse!", etc., 895-903). Here where his rhetoric becomes more empty than effective, we return to the Pardoner as simoniac and exhibitor of fake relics, fully deserving of the Host's obscene (and very funny) repudiation:

Thou woldest make me kisse thyn olde breech
[underpants],
And swere it were a relyk of a seint,
Though it were with thy fundament [anus]
depeint! [painted] [948-950]

With the old man of the tale, however, the tone is much more sombre. The old man in the Pardoner's version of the exemplum is more of a mystery than his equivalent in the analogues, where he shows the rioters the way to the gold, while refusing it himself. In 'The Pardoner's Tale' he has a story of his own. He is "forwrapped" save for his face (718), as though already in his shroud.

Though he is free to wander over the earth, he is a "restelees kaityf" [captive] (728) who cannot die:

And on the ground, which is my moodres

> *[mother's] gate,*
> *I knokke with my staf bothe erly and late,*
> *And seye, 'Leeve [beloved] mooder, leet me in!*
> *[729-731]*

Since the Pardoner has given him a story, it's tempting to take the old man as a figure for the Pardoner himself. He is not just the Old Man in Ephesians 4.22, whom St Paul enjoins us to put behind us, but someone even more radically self-alienated than that. As Patterson suggests, he is Cain, who "must wander because the earth, having been polluted by his brother's blood, now refuses to receive him". Cain's personal equivalent in the New Testament is Judas, who medieval exegetes judged had sinned more greatly in hanging himself than in betraying Christ. The old man is the Pardoner's own denial of redemption. His un-accommodated state stands for the Pardoner's despair.

Chaucer's use of language

By the end of the tenth century the language spoken in the South of England was a form of Anglo-Saxon now called Late West Saxon. Anglo-Saxon resembled German more than it did modern English. The Norman Conquest of 1066 saw two fundamental cultural changes in English life: first, government became centralised in

London; second, society became a hierarchy in which the aristocrats and other elites spoke French, while the common people continued to speak English. So the class divide was reinforced by a linguistic barrier.

At the time Chaucer was born in 1343, schools taught children to speak and do all their lessons in French. As a child of the mercantile upper-middle class, Chaucer would therefore have spoken French from an early age. And he would have continued to use that language when, as a teenager in 1357, he became a page to Elizabeth de Burgh, Countess of Ulster. She was the wife of Lionel, Duke of Clarence, the second surviving son of Edward III and John of Gaunt's brother. So when Chaucer became a squire at the court of Edward III and then Richard II, the promotion came naturally.

In the 1360s, as Derek Pearsall points out in his *Life of Geoffrey Chaucer*, the court was predominantly French speaking. Philippa, Edward III's queen, was French, and a large part of the French royal family were staying in London, too, at that time, including Jean le Bon (John II of France), who had been taken prisoner at Poitiers. He was a patron of Machaut and Petrarch, and, according to Pearsall, "brought French artists and poets in his train to England, as well as French books".

Even then, though (Pearsall again), "there was

a good deal of interchange between English and French in court and aristocratic circles... Edward III no doubt spoke English with his military commanders and soldiers, and French with his Hainault born Queen and her retinue." By this time also the Parisian French favoured at court had diverged a long way from the Norman French spoken now largely in the provinces.

French had been the language of government as had Latin in the law courts, but in 1362, according to the Harvard Chaucer website's 'The English Language in the Fourteenth Century: The Status of English', "Parliament was opened with a speech by the Chief Justice in English (and by the Chancellor in the next two parliaments), the first time since the Conquest the native language was so used." Even more momentous, in that same

CHAUCER'S AUDIENCE

Chaucer clearly had a sense of an audience. The tales told on the way to Canterbury prompt reactions, not always welcome, from the other pilgrims, though whatever meanings emerge from the dialectic are not always a reliable guide to readers' responses.

But, Kathy Cawsey argues that this sense went far deeper than the exchanges in *The Canterbury Tales*. "His main works all contain embedded audiences," she writes in *Twentieth-Century*

year the law was opened to English speakers, when "Parliament enacted the Statute of Pleading, which called for 'All pleas which shall be pleaded in his [the King's] courts whatsoever, before any of his justices whatsoever... [to be] pleaded, shewed, defended, answered, debated, and judged in the English tongue.'"

By the 1380s, when Chaucer began to write *The Canterbury Tales*, English had replaced French as the medium of instruction in the primary schools. By 1385 the grammar schools had switched from teaching the construing of Latin from French to English. Richard II was a native English speaker, and although he "spoke and read French very well", according to the medieval historian Jean Froissart, it was as a second language.

In fact the 1380s could be described as the

Chaucer Criticism: Reading Audiences. His narrators are audiences in their own right, as they interact with the *auctores* on whose work they draw, like Boethius, Cicero and Boccaccio. Cawsey proposes the idea of an "audience function", a counterpart of Michel Foucault's "author function". Here's how it works: "In the same way that interpretation can be limited with reference to the author (what he could have known, could have thought, or was likely to have written), interpretation is also limited with reference to the audience (what they would know, how they would read/hear, how they would experience the text, how they would interpret ambiguity or irony or humour)."

As for Chaucer's actual audience, these were "royalty, lords lay and spiritual, great

decade of the great English vernacular movement. It was between 1382 and 1395 that the first great translation of the Latin Vulgate Bible was undertaken by John Wyclffe, Nicholas of Hereford, John Purvey and others, a text so widely used that it still survives in more than 250 manuscripts. This work was inspired by and further promoted the Lollard movement, a sortof English proto-Reformation advocating reform of the temporal wealth and secular concerns of the clerical orders, emphasising the authority of scripture over church ritual and questioning the literal transubstantiation of the Eucharist into the body and blood of Christ.

"It is very likely," writes Brenda Deen Schildgen, "that Chaucer, an associate of John of Gaunt, one of the most ardent supporters of the English language program, followed the

---

ladies and minor members of the court such as squires, pages, ladies in waiting and clerks, as well as more substantial men of the city", according to D. W. Robertson in *Chaucer's London*. "They would have had regular exposure to sermons working exegetically on texts, also to stained glass and statues moralizing episodes in scripture, or at least illustrating them

symbolically."

In other words, as Derek Pearsall puts it, we need "to look beyond the immediate entourage of the king and his nobility to the multitude of household knights and officials, diplomats and civil servants, who constituted the 'court' in its wider sense, that is, the national administration and its metropolitan milieu. It is here that we find men whose

intellectual and political debates about the translation project."

And so it was Chaucer who first exploited the English language in all its diversity. "Chaucer's poetry, in its bulk and quality, is the main evidence for this change" from French to English, writes Pearsall, "its main product, and perhaps even its main precipitant".

This claim that Chaucer's work not only reflected this linguistic transition but may have assisted in bringing it about seems astonishing at first glance, but given the range and originality of his literary output, perhaps no more so than the commonplace that Dante's poetry consolidated the Florentine vernacular as the norm for modern Italian.

But Chaucer had one advantage over Dante.

known interests and known association with Chaucer make them apt candidates for a 'Chaucer circle'".

And the audience for *The Canterbury Tales*? It can be imagined, writes Pearsall, as "a miscellaneous company of lettered London men, to be appropriately scandalized and delighted by the Wife of Bath and the fabliaux".

In *Chaucer and the Subject of History* Lee Patterson puts the issue more schematically. "All of Chaucer's pre-*Canterbury Tales* poetry was almost certainly written within the environment of noble and royal courts and was directed to a court audience," he says. However, the modest format and wide circulation of *The Canterbury Tales* manuscripts show that the later work reached audiences well beyond the original courtly circle ■

His vernacular contains not one but three vocabularies: Anglo-Saxon, French and Latin, or those of the Anglo-Saxons, their Norman invaders and the terminology of the church and law to which both communities subscribed. And because of the Norman Conquest, the first two were assigned different cultural values. Roughly speaking, the French half gives us our 'cultivated' terms and the Anglo-Saxon our 'natural' words. So we have 'cow', 'sheep' and 'pig' for the animals in the barnyard, but 'beef', 'mutton' and 'pork' for what goes on the table. (If you run a restaurant, try putting 'hot sheep' or 'boiled cow' on your menu, then sit back in front of a mirror so you can watch yourself go broke.)

Beyond this contrast between raw and cooked lie the inalienable legal and governmental terms, like 'jury', 'judge', 'court', and 'parliament' – all derived from Norman-French because it's they who were in charge. But there are no fewer than three synonyms relating to the man at the very top: the Anglo-Saxon 'kingly', French 'royal' and Latin 'regal'.

Manuals of English style often favour the Anglo-Saxon side of our vocabulary on the grounds that it is usually more 'concrete' and less 'abstract'. As an example of the sort of 'abstract roundabout' to be avoided, Sir Ernest Gowers, author of Plain Words (1948) offers this typical civil-service-ese pronouncement: "Food consumption has been dominated by the world supply situation", for which he offers the improved: "People have had to eat what they could get."

In his essay 'Politics and the English Language' (1946) George Orwell famously re-wrote Ecclesiastes 9.11 ("I returned, and saw under the sun, that the race is not to the swift, nor the battle to the strong, neither yet bread to the wise") as:

> Objective consideration of contemporary phenomena compels the conclusion that success or failure in competitive activities exhibits no tendency to be commensurate with innate capacity.

What's noticeable in both samples is that the 'bad' abstractions are also words of Latin/French origin, if only for the simple reason that most of our abstract vocabulary comes from that source of our language.

Or rather, it was the 'establishment' word that prevailed for the relevant abstract idea. In *How We'd Talk if the English had Won in 1066* (2009) David Cowley exhibits plenty of Anglo-Saxon abstract terms long since lost, like *fleshbesmittingness* for the state of being smitten by the flesh, or (as we say, post-1066) 'carnal attraction'. Or *unmetefastnesse* for 'excess' or 'intemperance'. Or *tharfednesse* for 'poverty' or 'destitution'. In fact, with their –*ness* ending the

Anglo-Saxons could fabricate all the abstract nouns they needed, just as modern Germans can with their –*heit* suffix.

Where words from both (or all three) sources have survived side by side into modern English, it could be because they, like the words for raw and cooked animals, have come to take on different stylistic tones. 'Infant', 'child' and 'kid' may share the same dictionary meaning, but the first is slightly 'posher' and/or literary than the (relatively neutral) second, and the third is slangy. Or the meanings themselves may differ slightly. Take 'sight' and 'vision', for example. The latter might imply moral, intellectual or imaginative powers that are out of the present visual range. Or with 'till' and 'cultivate': the former is normally confined to the physical act of digging over the soil, whereas the latter is usually taken metaphorically, to mean 'to improve by labour or study', 'to develop a skill in' or even 'to seek the society of' or 'make friends with'. And so on.

Chaucer exploited the full tonal and lexical range of the vernacular: formal and French for terms of chivalry in courtly romances like "Troilus and Criseyde" (early 1380s), declarative and Latin for the sound practical theology of 'The Parson's Tale', informal and English for tales drawn from contemporary life.

And even in *The Canterbury Tales*, normally so attentive to the accents, rhythms and lexical range of everyday speech, there are places where ordinary expression won't do. In 'The Knight's Tale' Palamon complains to the goddess Fortune after he realises that Arcite, his rival for the love of Emily, has been released from prison, and is therefore at liberty to woo her actively:

> *What governaunce is in this prescience*
> *That giltelees tormenteth innocence?*
> *And yet encresseth this al my penaunce,*
> *That man is bounden to his observaunce.*
>
> *[1313-1316]*

This high style is not merely atmospheric – not, that is, just there to add to the solemnity of the drama – but absolutely mandated by its subject matter, itself derived from Chaucer's translation of Boethius's sixth-century philosophical work, the *Consolation of Philosophy*, originally published in Latin. Those words ending in '–nce' are an essential part of our abstract vocabulary. Try rewriting that paragraph in words selected exclusively from the Anglo-Saxon branch of the English language, and you have to resort to monstrosities like *bilewhiteness*, *deedboteness*, and *boldness*, for 'innocence', 'penaunce' and 'observance'.

But it was the double (and occasionally treble) vocabularies of English – that contrast between the 'high', formal and French-derived parlance of the court and the 'low', informal, Anglo-Saxon speech of the common man and woman – that Chaucer would explore and exploit for a huge range of ironies and a whole new field of satirical effects. And nowhere is the contrast so well set out than at the beginnings of 'The Knight's Tale' and 'The Miller's Tale':

> *Whilom, as olde stories tellen us,*
> *Ther was a duc that highte [was called]*
> *Theseus ...*
>
> *[859-860]*

> *Whilhom ther was dwellynge at Oxenford*
> *A riche gnof [lout], that geestes [lodgers] heeld*
> *to board ...*
>
> *[3187-3188]*

Not to mention their endings:

> *And thus with alle blisse and melodye*
> *Hath Palamon ywedded Emelye...*
> *And Emelye hym loveth so tenderly,*
> *And he hire serveth so gentilly,*
> *That nevere was no word hem [them] bitwene*
> *Of jalousie or any oother teene [vexation],*
> *Thus endeth Palamon and Emelye;*
> *And God save al this faire compaignye!*
> *Amen.*
>
> *[3097-3108]*

Thus swyved [fucked] was this carpenteris wyf,
For al his kepyng [guarding] and his jalousye,
And Absolon hath kist her nether ye [lower eye]
And Nicholas is scalded on the towte [arse].
This tale is doon, and God save al the rowte!
                                    [crowd] [3850-3854]

The point to notice here is simply the range of English words at Chaucer's disposal, and the widely differing moral and social values they entail.

But for Chaucer language was not just a medium; it was a theme in its own right. He was fascinated by true and false preaching, by the match or mismatch between the morality of the man and the soundness or otherwise of his doctrinal message. The Parson and the Pardoner are the obvious polarities, but the acrimonious debate between the Friar and the Summoner reveals a wide range of preacher's abuses. Behind this concern, as Carolyn Dinshaw explains in her seminal essay, 'Eunuch Hermeneutics', lay the widespread anxiety that language had fallen along with mankind when Adam and Eve ate the apple. Though redeemed with the sacrifice of Christ – the word restored to the Word – language remained insufficient to express the divine. The problem is compounded when language is used to tell stories. "Made of flawed language," Dinshaw writes, "fiction is not literally true... but it plays on our desire for truth."

So the text of *The Canterbury Tales* generates lots of interest in *how* people speak in public, especially when telling stories, how their sometimes self-consciously elaborate rhetorical flights contrast with other aspects (including the moral) of their discourse. This discrepancy is acute with the Pardoner, the Friar and the Summoner. By the time you reach this point in 'The Pardoner's Tale'...

> *O cursed synne of alle cursednesse!*
> *O traytours homycide, O wikkednesse!*
> *O glotonye, luxurie [lechery], and hasardry!*
> *[gambling] [895-898]*

you know it's time to start counting the silver. But even the Franklin, though comparatively benign, sets out to dazzle with his rhetoric, even while disclaiming any expertise in the art:

> *I learned nevere rethorik, certeyn:*
> *Thyng that I speke, it moot be bare and pleyn.*
> *[719-720]*

But don't be fooled. This is itself a rhetorical figure, the inability *topos*, or 'unaccustomed-as-I-am-to-public-speaking' trope. He uses it more extensively in line 1266, where he says "I ne kan [do not know] no termes of astrologye", but then goes on to speak of "tables Tolletanes" (astrological tables from Toledo, 1273), "the eighte speere [sphere]" and how far the constellation Alnath was advanced from the head of Aries (1280-1283).

Yet for all that, the Franklin is not entirely secure in his rhetoric. When he displays an ambitious figure for nightfall – "For th'orisonte [horizon] hath reft [taken from] the sonne his lyght" – he can't count on his audience's understanding of this epic formula, so has to add quickly, "This is as muche to seye as it was nyght" (1017-1018). Read (or spoken) together, the lines form a comically bathetic couplet.

1335 Giovanni Boccaccio, *Il Filostrato*, source of *Troilus and Criseyde*.

Some time between 1340 and 1345 Chaucer is born into a prosperous London family, his father is a vintner, his mother an extensive property owner.

1339 Boccaccio begins *Il Teseide*, source of 'The Knight's Tale'.

1346 English victory at Crecy

1348-50 The Black Death

1349-51 Boccaccio's *Decameron*

1357 Chaucer becomes a page in the household of Elizabeth de Burgh, Countess of Ulster.

1359 Edward III invades France; Chaucer serves in the army.

1360 Chaucer captured during the siege of Reims; the king ransoms him for £16.

1366 Chaucer marries Philippa Roet, a lady-in-waiting to Edward III's queen, Philippa of Hainault.

1367 Their son Thomas is born.

1367 Chaucer becomes a varlet de chambre, and later a squire in the court of Edward III; granted a payment of 20 marks per annum for life.

1367-70 The text of Langland, 'Piers Plowman'

1368-72 Chaucer translates part of *Romaunt of the Rose*, and writes *The Book of the Duchess*, in honour of Blanche of Lancaster, late wife of John of Gaunt, who died in 1369.

1369 Chaucer serves with John of Gaunt's army in France.

1372 Chaucer's wife Philippa in the household of John of Gaunt's second wife, Constance

1373 Chaucer in Genoa and Florence on a diplomatic mission, where he may have met Francesco Petrarch and Boccaccio

1374 Chaucer is appointed to the important post of comptroller of the customs for the Port of London; death of Petrarch.

1375 Death of Boccaccio

1377 Edward III dies; Richard II becomes king.

1378 Richard II sends Chaucer to Italy on a secret diplomatic mission to the English mercenary Sir John Hawkwood, a possible model for the Knight in The Canterbury Tales.

1380 Birth of Chaucer's son Lewis; Chaucer writes The Parliament of Fowls; Cecilia Chaumpaigne signs an affidavit releasing Chaucer from all actions in the case 'de raptu meo'.

1381 The Peasants' Revolt

1382-86 Chaucer writes *Boece* and *Troilus and Criseyede.*

1382 English translations of the Bible begin to
appear in stages at the instigation of John Wycliffe.

1385 Chaucer moves to Kent, where he serves as
Justice of the Peace from 1385 to 1389.

1385-87 Chaucer writes The Legend of Good
Women, and 'Palamoun and Arcite', later used as 'The Knight's
Tale'.

1386 Chaucer returned as Member of Parliament for Kent.

1387 Conjectured date of the death of Philippa, Chaucer's wife

1387-90 John Gower's Confessio Amantis.

1387-92 Chaucer begins *The Canterbury Tales*

1389 Chaucer is appointed clerk of the works at
Westminster, Tower of London, and other royal estates.

1392-95 Chaucer completes most of *The Canterbury Tales*

1394 King Richard II grants Chaucer an annuity of
20 pounds a year,

1396-1400 Chaucer writes the last of *The Tales*, including 'The
Nun's Priest's Tale' and 'The Parson's Tale'.

1399 Richard II is deposed by Henry Bolingbroke, son of John
of Gaunt; as king, Henry renews Chaucer's royal annuities,
though there is some doubt as to whether these were ever paid.

1400 Chaucer's dies and is buried in Westminster
Abbey.

FURTHER READING

Getting started

www.courses.fas.harvard.edu/~chaucer/
This Harvard Geoffrey Chaucer Website offers an excellent
introduction to the basics, with an extensive bibliography, a
selection of sources, extracts of major critical readings, essays
on Chaucer's life and his language, on pilgrimage, courtly love,
medieval science and other topics, plus a tutorial on Chaucer's
pronunciation, grammar and vocabulary.

Texts

Larry D. Benson, et al, ed., *The Riverside Chaucer*, third edition,
Oxford: Oxford University Press, 2008
The authoritative text of Chaucer's complete works.

Geoffrey Chaucer, *The Canterbury Tales: Fifteen Tales and the
General Prologue*, ed. V. A. Kolve and Glending Olson, the
Norton Critical Edition, New York: W.W. Norton & Company,
2005
Contains the major tales, set out in highly readable fashion, with
glosses in the margins instead of buried at the bottom of the page;
also includes a selection of sources and critical essays.

The Bible

Chaucer's Bible was the Latin Vulgate, the most accessible
English version of which is the Douay/Rheims version
translation, first published in 1582 and 1609. New York: P. J.
Kennedy and Sons, 1914

Kevin J. Vanhoozer, ed., *Dictionary for Theological Interpretation of the Bible.* Grand Rapids, MI: Baker Book House, 2005)

Chaucer's life and work

Derek Pearsall, *The Life of Geoffrey Chaucer: A Critical Biography.* Oxford: Blackwell, 1992
On balance the best – and best written – critical biography.

Sources

Guillaume de Lorris and Jean de Meun, *The Romance of the Rose,* trans. Charles Dahlberg. Princeton: Princeton University Press, 1971
Translated in part as Chaucer's Romaunt of the Rose, this monumental work suffused and inspired much of Chaucer's literary production.

N. R. Havely, ed., *Chaucer's Boccaccio: Sources for Troilus, the Knight's and Franklin's Tales.* Chaucer Studies V. Cambridge: D S. Brewer, 1980
Explores Chaucer's debt to Boccaccio's *Il Decamerone, Il Filocolo* and *La Teseide.*

Leonard Michael Koff, Branda Deed Schildgen, eds., *The Decameron and the Canterbury Tales: New Essays on an Old Question.* Cranbury, N. J., London and Mississuaga, Ont.: Associated University Presses, 2000
Includes Brenda Deen Schildgen, 'Boethius and the Consolation of Literature in Boccaccio's Decameron and Chaucer's Canterbury Tales'.

Critical casebooks

Valerie Allen and Ares Axiotis, eds., *New Casebooks: Chaucer.* London: Macmillan, Palgrave, 1997
Contains essays discussed in this book, like Barrie Ruth Straus,

'The Subversive Discourse of the Wife of Bath: Phallocentric
Discourse and the Imprisonment of Criticism'; Monica
McAlpine, 'The Pardoner's Homosexuality and How it Matters';
Gerald Morgan, 'Boccaccio's *Filocolo* and the Moral Argument
of **The Franklin's Tale**'.

Lee Patterson, ed., *Geoffrey Chaucer's The Canterbury Tales: A
Casebook*. Oxford: Oxford University Press, 2007
Includes essays discussed in this book, like Harry Berger, Jr.,
'Pleasure and Responsibility in The Franklin's Tale' and V. A.
Kolve, 'Nature, Youth, and Nowell's Flood'.

Critical history
Kathy Cawsey, *Twentieth-Century Chaucer Criticism: Reading
Audiences*. Farnham, Surrey and Burlington, Vermont: Ashgate,
2011
An insightful survey of the major critical movements from
Kittredge to Patterson.

Major critical movements, listed chronologically
George Lyman Kittredge, *Chaucer and his Poetry*. Cambridge,
MA: Harvard University Press, 1915
Reading *The Canterbury Tales* as a dramatic exchange between
characters, Kittredge famously perceived a debate about
marriage as between the Wife of Bath, the Clerk and the
Merchant over the question of whether the wife or husband
should exert control, a conflict to be resolved by the Franklin,
with of his tale of a husband who pledges to be 'servant in love.
and lord in mariage'.

C. S. Lewis, *The Allegory of Love*. Oxford: The Clarendon Press,
1936
Lewis touches *The Canterbury Tales* mainly at the point of
'The Knight's Tale', because his centre of interest is Chaucer's
romances, for which he sees the elaborate conventions of courtly

love as a serious figurative language for exploring the complexities of love in a field of forces like nature and fortune.

Charles Muscatine, *Chaucer and the French Tradition.* Berkeley: University of CaliforniaPress, 1957
In his finely written book Muscatine takes the search for Chaucer's sources beyond content into form and style, finding echoes of French courtly and bourgeois literature in Chaucer's work. The work still stands as one of the best close readings of the Chaucer text.

D.W. Robertson Jr., *A Preface to Chaucer: Studies in Medieval Perspectives*. Princeton: Princeton University Press, 1958
According to Robertson, Chaucer's readers were well enough versed in exegetical and symbolic traditions as represented in the sermons, liturgy and iconography of the churches they attended to sense the ironic distance between a courtly love romance (say) and the true path to salvation. For Robertson all *The Canterbury Tales* are moral allegories with the same anagogical meaning.

E. Talbot Donaldson, *Speaking of Chaucer.* London: The Athlone Press, 1970
Donaldson brought the New Criticism to bear on *The Canterbury Tales,* arguing above all for an ironic distance between Chaucer the author and Chaucer the pilgrim telling the stories.

Caroline Dinshaw, *Chaucer's Sexual Politics*, Madison: University of Wisconsin Press, 1989
This, the first full-length feminist study of Chaucer, distinguishes between reading like a man and like a woman, in terms not only of the critics but also of Chaucer's characters themselves.

Lee Patterson, *Chaucer and the Subject of History.* Madison: University of Wisconsin Press, 1991

In place of the old historical readings of Chaucer (Lewis's courtly love, Robertson's hermeneutics and iconography of medieval Christianity), Patterson offers new historicist contexts, like the Wife of Bath considered against the role and social position of wealthy widows or the Pardoner against the increasing importance placed on confession and penance following the Fourth Lateran Council.

Narrative and interpretation

Patrick J. Gallagher and Helen Damico, eds., *Hermeneutics and Medieval Culture*. Albany: State University Press of New York, 1989

Alastair Minnis, *Fallible Authors: Chaucer's Pardoner and Wife of Bath*. Philadelphia: University of Pennsylvania Press, 2008
Takes an interesting line about immoral 'authors' – that is, tellers of tales – who tell moral stories, as contextualised in Medieval auctor theory.

Sabine Volk-Birke, *Chaucer and Medieval Preaching: Rhetoric for Listeners in Sermons and Poetry*. Tübingen: Gunter Narr Verlag, 1991

Specific tales

C. David Benson, "Chaucer's Pardoner: His Sexuality and Modern Critics", Medievalia 8 (1985 [for 1982]), 337-46.

Richard Firth Green, "The Sexual Normality of Chaucer's Pardoner" Medievalia 8 (1985 [for 1982]), 351-57.

David Raybin and Linda Tartt Holley, eds., *Closure in The Canterbury Tales: The Role of the Parson's Tale.* Kalamazoo: Medieval Institute Publications, 2000

INDEX

141

First published in 2014 by
Connell Guides
8th Floor, Friars Bridge Court
Blackfriars Road
London SE1 8NZ
10 9 8 7 6 5 4 3 2 1

Picture credits:

p.19 © Rex Features
p.27 © 'The Canterbury Tales' film poster. Courtesy Everett Collection/REX
pp.35, 57 & 76-77 © Canterbury Tales mural by Ezra Winter (1886–1949).
North Reading Room, west wall, Library of Congress John Adams Building,
Washington, D.C. Photographed 2007 by Carol Highsmith (1946–).
pp.56, 57, 69 & 109 © The Canterbury Pilgrims, 1810, by William Blake.
Copper engraving printed on paper. 5th state, printed c. 1820-23. Courtesy of
the Charles Deering McCormick Library of Special Collections, Northwestern
University.
p.90 © The Decameron, 1916, by John William Waterhouse. Courtesy
National Museums Liverpool (Lady Lever Art Gallery).

A CIP catalogue record for this book is available from the British Library.
ISBN 978-1-907776-25-0

Design © Nathan Burton
Assistant Editors:
Matthew Conroy, Katie Sanderson & Pierre Smith Khanna
Printed in Great Britain by Butler, Tanner and Dennis

www.connellguides.com